TWENTY WEALDEN WALKS FOR NATURALISTS AND RAMBLERS

incorporating an appreciation of the botanical, zoological and historical richness of bridlepaths and footpaths.

A University of Sussex, Centre for Continuing Education, Occasional Paper.

Edited by John Feltwell

PREFACE

The idea for this book has been born out of the mass of data accumulated on adult education field trips carried out under the auspices of the Centre for Continuing Education at the University of Sussex and the wide experience of the editor with similar walkabouts for the other universities of Kent, London and Surrey.

Practical contact with the environment is a necessity to the understanding of the ramifications of nature and is always eagerly awaited by students after their twenty-week winter classes. All serious naturalists write down their observations as there is so much to absorb and the human mind is always enormously forgetful.

This occasional paper, therefore, has three aims; first, to capture some of the exciting and unexpected finds we had during our field trips in 1982; second, to introduce potential CCE students into the rich rewards of pursuing outdoor activities; and, third, to see how we set about the detailed study of the richness of bridlepaths and footpaths.

By itself the paper should stand as a guide to some interesting walks to be had in the Sussex countryside, all within 25 miles of Brighton.

ACKNOWLEDGEMENTS

Many people have helped in the production of this paper. The Centre for Continuing Education at the University of Sussex has provided the opportunity for this to appear in their on-going series of OCCASIONAL PAPERS. Special thanks are due to John Lowerson, Fred Gray and Betty Catling for helpful discussion and reading of the various drafts. Members of the editor's natural history classes which have been taught in the towns of Battle, Hastings, Rottingdean, Rye, Wadhurst and on the 'Brain Train' (the classes held on commuter trains to London) have provided much first-hand information.

Mr. John Midgley (Battle) contributed research on the origins of bridlepaths and footpaths; Mr. David Turner (Battle) drew all the pencil drawings of the animals, fungi and habitats and Mrs. Sheila Lawrence (Wadhurst) drew the close-up studies of the mosses from her local wood. Written contributions on field notes and species lists were compiled by Mrs. Joan Tate and Miss Vera Barren (Tunbridge Wells). All the black and white photographs were supplied by John Feltwell's "Wildlife Matters" Photographic Library (Henley Down, Catsfield, East Sussex). The maps were prepared for publication by Mary Lowerson and the manuscript typed by Betty Hayde.

The editor is indebted to the hundreds of adult education students who have made all these studies possible and who have mutually supported this work through discussion and participation.

(Dr) John Feltwell, FRES, FLS, MIBiol.
Part-time tutor for the
Centre for Continuing Education,
University of Sussex,
Falmer,
BRIGHTON,
East Sussex.

October 1982.

CONTENTS

BRIDLEPATHS

WALK	1	Cross in Hand to Old Mill Farm, Heathfield
WALK	2	Crowborough
WALK	3	Darwell Reservoir
WALK	4	Haysden Water
WALK	5	Horse Eye Level, Pevensey
WALK	6	Jevington
WALK	7	Penhurst, Catsfield
WALK	8	Swife to Punnett's Town
WALK	9	Iden Wood, Rye Foreign
WALK	10	The Ridge to Coghurst, Hastings.

FOOTPATHS

WALK	11	Abbot's Wood, Polegate
WALK	12	Beachy Head Nature Trail
WALK	13	Brightling
WALK	14	Footlands Wood, Battle
WALK	15	Forest Way, Hartfield
WALK	16	Great Wood, Battle
WALK	17	Octavia Hill Woodland
WALK	18	Rushlake Green
WALK	19	Cuckmere and Seaford Head
WALK	20	500 acre wood, Ashdown Forest

BIBLIOGRAPHY AND USEFUL ADDRESSES

INTRODUCTION

Current awareness in the environment is increasing at an astonishing rate. People are becoming more interested in our living heritage - or what is left of it - and this is reflected, not least of all, in the popularity of continuing education classes in the natural sciences, which are well attended by people from all age groups.

It was through discussion of the relative and comparative richness of the flora and fauna of bridlepaths and footpaths that it was mutually agreed to walk a selection of these in the Weald, whilst at the same time to look at nature reserves and other places of interest locally as part of our classes. Forestry Commission plantations and nature trails received our attention and raised the question of relative species-richness of deciduous and evergreen woodlands. Which type of woodlands would you expect to have a richer variety of wildlife? Therefore, in this book you will find an appreciation of the richness of bridlepaths and footpaths and comments on the natural history interest of the various habitats that we visited.

Much of the countryside is greatly unused by the general public but yet it is criss-crossed by footpaths and bridlepaths which give everyone legal right of access. We encountered few walkers along our paths and in several places footpaths had been unwalked for so long that we had to fight our way through brambles and long vegetation, whilst in other places barbed wire hindered our progress and hedgerows had been removed so that on one occasion we were obliged to walk straight across a standing crop to keep to our legal right of way and not trespass around the edge of the field.

Our paths passed through farmsteads, fields of friendly bullocks (no bulls were encountered!), woodlands studded with bluebells and early purple orchids, orchards, open meadows, scrubby thickets, overgrown copses, and we caught sight of rabbits, kestrels, herons, Canada geese, saw deer slots, found badger setts, wild bees in hollow trees, butterflies, day-flying moths as well as masses of spring-time flowers, fungi and trees. Our hedge-dating revealed some interesting facts and figures along the bridlepaths we walked and our minds went riot with thoughts of what it was like in earlier centuries along these very paths - of hay wagons passing along the wide grassy bridlepaths, of muddy tracks and of domestic animals being driven to market.

The hedgerows were dated using the well-established principle that it takes about one hundred years to establish one new species along a hedgerow; thus thirty-yard samples of hedgerow were examined for woody species and the average taken. If six woody species were recorded on average from a minimum of three samples this would indicate that the hedgerow was about 600 years old. We have presented some of this information in the form of tables.

Bridlepaths enable the naturalist to see the heart of England's countryside. They are usually wider, better defined and freer from obstruction than ordinary footpaths, yet they take the public well away from modern traffic and often perpetuate the routes taken by those on horseback and on foot centuries ago. Bridlepaths traverse what were the forests of the Forest of the Weald or <u>Anderida</u>, whose timber was later to fuel the Sussex iron industry; they follow roads made by the Romans long since lost but for the indication provided by the bridlepaths themselves; and they march over the Downs along trackways dating back to the days of ancient man keeping aloof from wild animals of the forests and the malarial mosquito.

Public bridlepaths are a form of public highway; the Wildlife and Countryside Act of 1981 states that the public has a right of way over them on foot and on horseback. An earlier Act of 1968 provides that cyclists may use them as well, but they must give way to other users. Normally the width of a public bridlepath is undefined, though Parliament prescribes that any gate across it must be at least five feet wide.

Few people will fail to be rewarded by the sense of discovery offered by bridlepaths: of different routes, of new vistas, and of flora and fauna - some thriving well away from today's chemicals, others trying to avoid extinction: they are often to be found within a few hundred yards of the surfaced road or overpopulated picnic areas. All one needs to be is inquisitive, observant and well-shod.

The origins of bridlepaths are certainly obscure but, judging by their floristic richness, they appear to go back many hundreds of years; in fact, close to a thousand years in some cases. Our initial presumption that bridlepaths were more interesting biologically than footpaths proved to be well-founded. Bridlepaths in any case generally provide a much bigger habitat and refuge for plants and animal than footpaths as they often have two hedgerows enclosing a grassy tack and were used for domestic and agricultural thoroughfare (Figure 1). The width of the bridlepath would have been sufficient in many cases for horse-drawn farm vehicles to pass.

One noticeable feature of bridlepaths which we discovered were the delightful sunken lanes wherever they passed down the typical Sussex ghylls. In the winter rains the muds and sands would run down the tracks cutting away at the banks each year until the level of the path was much lower than the base of the hedge. Today some of these sunken tracks are so unpassable that secondary paths have been trodden along the banks of adjacent hedgerows, creating further extensions of the hedgerow habitat. Today, the sunken lanes are marvellously cool places which support lively collections of shade and damp-loving plants such as mosses and liverworts (<u>bryophytes</u>), ferns and fungi.

Bridlepaths were clearly used for riders as their name suggests and this is confirmed by the modern definition in the Oxford Dictionary 'fit for riders but not for vehicles'. Presumably some bridlepaths were used for horse-drawn vehicles as some of them are exceedingly wide, especially near farm buildings, but modern cars are now banned from using them.

Many of today's bridlepaths are those ancient thoroughfares which escaped the impact and permanence of tarmac. Several of the roads we motor along were old bridlepaths made good, but they have lost much of their interesting natural history appeal. Some of the bridlepaths probably fell into disuse through the decline of local industries, depopulation and increased use of major trunk roads. The Turnpike Act of 1663 presumably contributed to this but also encouraged use of minor roads and short-cuts through ghylls by those anxious to evade expensive tolls. Various acts since 1585 onwards sought to make the main users of these major roads - the ironmasters - pay for their upkeep. Certainly bridlepaths and footpaths were classified in the Enclosure Acts of the early nineteenth century.

Both G.K. Chesterton (1874-1936) and Rudyard Kipling (1865-1936), who lived in Sussex, first at Rottingdean and then at Burwash (Batemans), had words to say about our roads and paths; Chesterton in his 'The Rolling English Road' alludes to the twisting and winding nature of roads thus:

> The rolling English drunkard made the rolling English roads.
>
> A reeling road, a rolling road, that rambles round the shire;
>
> And after him the parson ran, the sexton and the squire,
>
> A merry road, a mazy road, and such as we do tread.

Kipling talks of the abandoned tracks in his 'The Way through the Woods':

> There was once a path through the woods,
>
> Before they planted the trees,
>
> It is underneath the coppice and heath,
>
> And the thin anemones.
>
> Only the keeper sees
>
> That, where the ring-dove broods,
>
> And the badgers roll at ease,
>
> There was once a road through the woods.

The Edwardian botanist, A.R. Horwood, writing at the turn of the century was clearly concerned about the deleterious effects of agriculture on wildlife and recognised the importance of hedgerows and wayside verges; 'These islets in a sea of otherwise purely artificial fields, meadows, woods, etc., are really to the far-seeing botanist the most interesting part of his quest or study.'

* * * * * *

FIGURE 1

DIAGRAM OF AERIAL VIEW OF BRIDLEPATH AND FOOTPATH

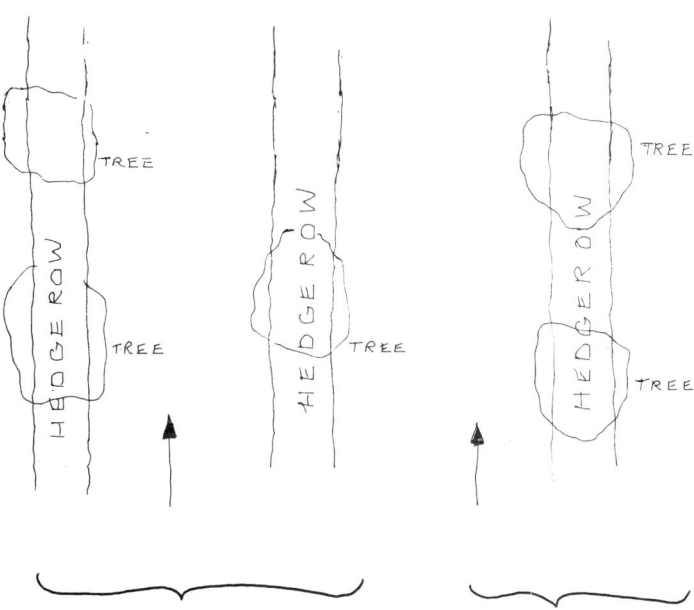

BRIDLEPATH

Often two hedges separated by a wide grassy track; thus twice the available hedgerow habitat of a footpath hedge.

FOOTPATH

One hedgerow with adjacent footpath.

THE MAPS

The bridlepath walks are clearly visible on all Ordnance Survey 1 : 50,000 Landranger maps as thick broken red lines and can be distinguished from footpaths which are thin broken red lines. The maps have been drawn with north roughly at the top of the page.

Most of the walks described are circular but they can of course be walked in the reverse direction. Three one-way walks are also described so for those it will be necessary to arrange suitable transport at either end.

BRIDLEPATHS

WALKS 1 - 10

WALK 1   CROSS IN HAND, TO OLD MILL FARM, HEATHFIELD

This is a one-way and downhill walk so it is necessary to leave your cars outside Old Mill Farm.

The start of the walk from the main A265 road outside Heathfield follows a tarmac road to Herrings Farm and passes through sweet chestnut coppice woodland with oak standards. The roadside hedge which appears very old is patchy with some ancient layered beech trees; it passes the very high radio mast which dominates Cross-in-Hand from a distance. The bridlepath also passes what appears to be a neglected vineyard which is in an exposed south-easterly aspect. There is plenty of evidence that iron ore was mined alongside the path as there are deep water-filled holes which have black murky bottoms.

Herring Farm is a rather solid and large farmhouse with a fairly clogged-up pond outside. The bridlepath passes through the middle of the farm buildings and between two barns which are used as hangars for at least five collectors' aeroplanes. A grass airstrip lies parallel with the bridlepath which at this place is very typical of a bridlepath and which looks fairly untouched, i.e. a wide grass expanse with two hedgerows. Here we decided to do a bit of hedge-dating and worked out that it must be of 1380 or thereabouts. We found 5, 7 and 8 species in our three 30 yard stretches indicating an average of 660 years of age. The hedge itself didn't look particularly old, it had been trimmed within recent years but was bushy and continuous throughout its length with an abundance of hazel.

After this exciting section of the bridlepath the path becomes obscure, broken and unwalkable as it descends into a sunken lane stretch invaded with scrub and bracken, and down to a tributary of the river Rother. At the bottom there is a very ricketty bridge over a very picturesque stream which is brightly-coloured orange with the iron ore deposits. One can almost hear the horse-drawn wagon being encouraged across this muddy bottom in those days when produce was being taken along this path. The banks of the stream were also covered in liverworts which contrasted with the orange deposits.

The path then passes up past some houses, over an old railway line supporting 20 year old vegetation including ash and bramble, through a 200 year old oakwood, down through another oak wood and out onto the road at Old Mill Farm.

WALK 1   CROSS IN HAND TO OLD MILL FARM, HEATHFIELD

O.S. MAP SHEET 199,

Starting point map reference : 566217

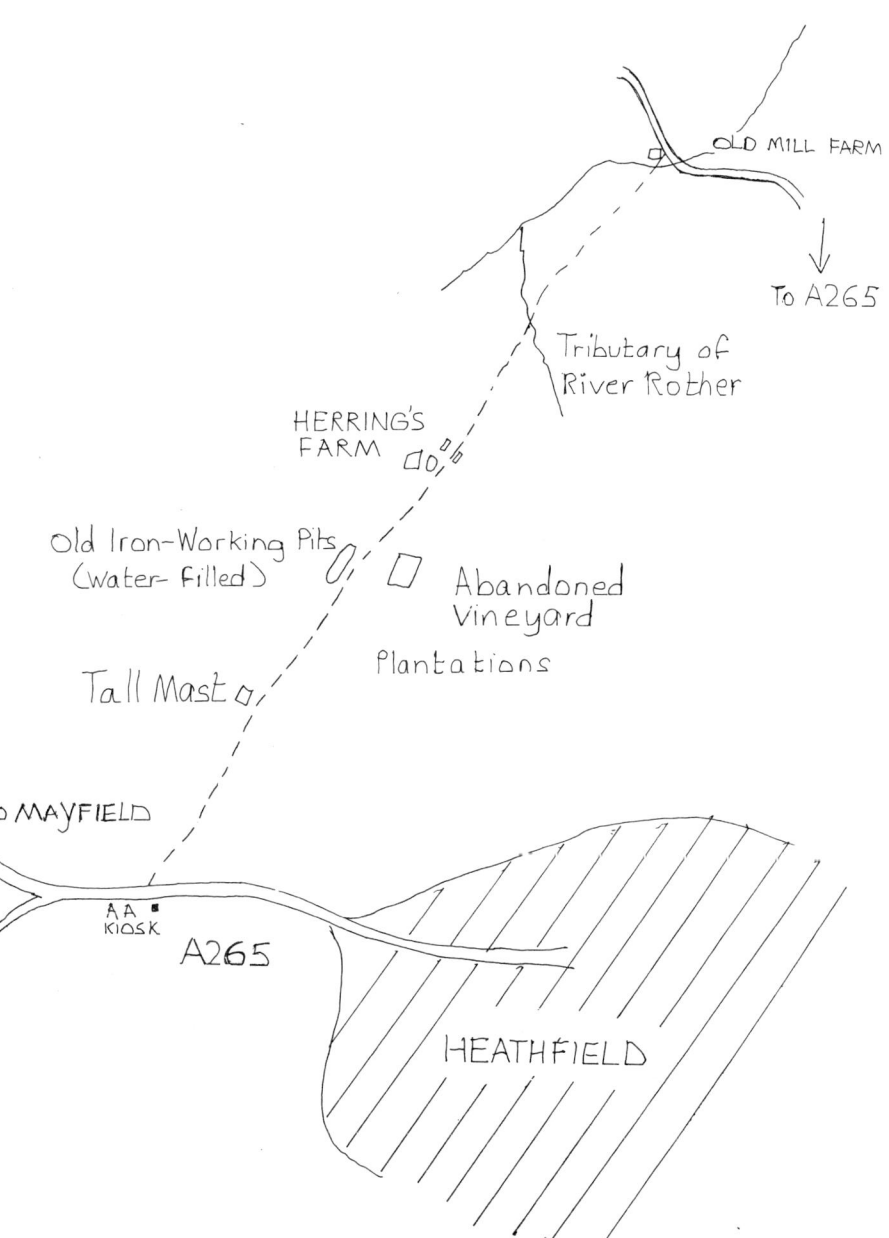

WALK 2   CROWBOROUGH

This turned out to be one of the best if not lengthy walks accomplished - probably over three miles or $2\frac{1}{2}$ hours at a leisurely naturalist's pace. At the start of the walk we set about a hedge dating and three of the 30 yard samples returned us 8,9 and 7 species in that order, i.e. an average of 8 or 800 years. This means that the hedge had been there since the twelfth century. It didn't look old because it had been cut down by hedgecutters to a metre and half, but looks can be deceiving. Overall there were about a dozen species present including yew which didn't come into our samples. The species we found were:

Woody Species	sample 1	sample 2	sample 3
Briar	+	+	+
Hawthorn	+	+	+
Hazel	+	+	+
Holly	+	+	+
Mountain Ash	+	+	+
Oak	+	+	+
Silver Birch	+	-	-
Apple	-	+	-
Maple	-	+	-
Sloe	+	+	+
Total species	8	9	7

The bridlepath progressed through to other farms past hedgerow banks with greater stitchwort, red campion, and yellow archangel and woods and coppices blue with bluebells. There were signs of badgers' tracks and a latrine but a sett was not immediately visible. Views to the north-west brought in at least three church spires on the horizon but we made no effort to identify them. The bridlepath dived down through neglected sweet chestnut coppice, past a 400 year old boundary oak (contemporary with the one at the start of the walk on the main road which has been pollarded and is hollow) - through clearings with carpets of bugle and yellow pimpernel and out across a small tributary of the Medway; here it is about one metre wide and one can jump across it. Speckled wood butterflies were flying about. Here the footpath has been obliterated by modern farming and instead of legally walking through the neat standing crop of corn and joining with another footpath which comes along at right angles, we trespassed by walking <u>around</u> the field. The footpath then passes through a small wood and we came across a colourful display of tall and healthy early purple orchids. The footpath now passes straight uphill to the main road but goes right through the middle of a farm where swallows were building in the sheds and past the front door of a cottage where an aviary full of canaries chatted away to us.

WALK 2   CROWBOROUGH

O.S. MAP SHEET 188

Starting point map reference : 513321

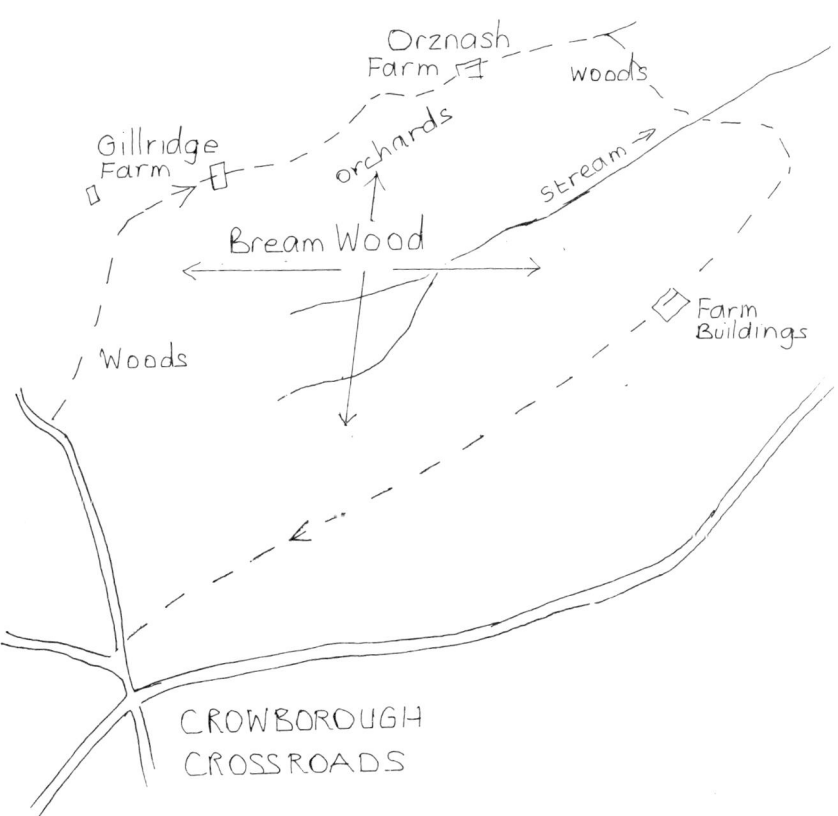

WALK 3   DARWELL RESERVOIR

Ample parking can be had at the official entrance to the Forestry Commission plantation where a notice warns of adders. This is a walk of about three miles and takes about 2½ hours. As there is so much plantation of larch and pine in the area it is probable that you will not see any of the reservoir until you are on the higher ground. The bridlepath is not marked and there is the distinct possibility that you will take the wrong forest track unless you can map-read properly. Nevertheless, shorter circular forest walks can be had within the plantation.

Along the rides there were plenty of common spotted orchids coming up in the boggy areas which supported spring cinquefoil and patches of delicate pink lousewort. Descending through the coppice woodland of ash, the ground was carpeted with bluebells and ramsons. Here the stream races noisily down to the reservoir almost like a highland stream. Progress can be made along the flat woods adjacent to the stream and in the glades there were plenty of green-veined white butterflies and twayblade orchids underfoot. Crossing the stream on the bridge by the aerial ropeway the bridlepath climbs uphill to recently-cut coppice chestnut woodland with oak standards. Here nightingales were heard and an adder seen on the path. Deer paths and slots were common in the mud, their paths clearly denoted through the dog's mercury.

Joining the road it is necessary to walk back to the entrance and this passes along lanes rich in early purple and common twayblade orchids.

WALK 3   DARWELL RESERVOIR

O.S. MAP SHEET 199

Starting point map reference : 695196

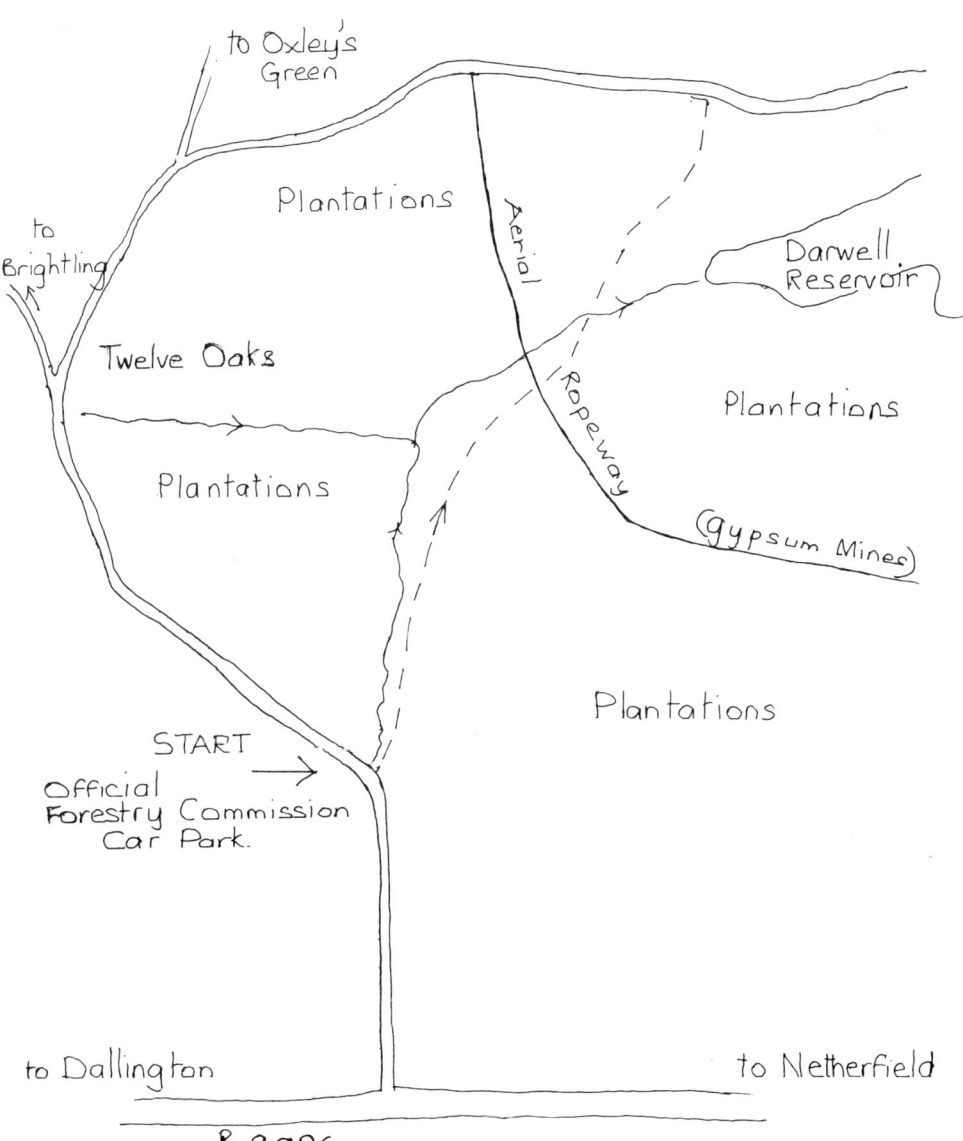

WALK 4 HAYSDEN WATER

This walk uses normal footpaths and passes the Haysden Water Nature Reserve owned by the Borough District of Tonbridge from whom permits can be obtained.

We set off northwards from Haysden along what looked like a very typical bridlepath, a grassy track with hedges both sides, but which was in fact a footpath. The hedges did not appear to be very old but the surprising thing which we found throughout was the abundance of hops climbing through the hedgerows. They may have been a hangover from periods when plenty of hop gardens were present but now no gardens could be seen.

Going westwards parallel with the railway we walked up and into the dry holding lake recently excavated to provide space for flood water for the Hildenborough barrage. The soil was supporting an interesting selection of plants in flower which included wild radish, celery-leaved buttercup, crosswort, ragwort and hemlock (leaves only). Small heath butterflies were already flying and a solitary comma was seen as well as a peacock and green-veined whites.

This walk takes in the Straight Mile - a very pleasant walk along a raised embankment which is probably of 300-400 years old judging by the magnificent oaks sporting fine boles. The barrage developments have taken away only about a third of the straight mile, but what is left is thick with wild flowers and those that were out included comfrey, white deadnettle and ground ivy.

A few Canada geese were present on the lake making noises and doing their head shaking, a sure sign of their displeasure with us. In the middle of the fields to the quieter western side of the lake there were groups of about 50 Canada geese, sometimes mixed with greylag geese, occupying the fields with bullocks. Occasionally the calls of geese wishing to joing their compatriots were heard - clearly they could not see each other because of the high hedges but were homed in by reciprocal calls. There was evidence along one of the paths back to Haysden that someone had been taking pot shots at the geese as there were .22 shotcases scattered about. One very surprising thing that we saw was a pair of fallow deer, one of which was a dark form, which were existing here in the large fields and thick hedgerows, probably as a splinter group of feral deer present throughout much of the Weald.

The bridlepaths around the Medway in this region are low-lying and it was not very surprising to find plenty of water-loving plants, such as Himalayan balsam, meadow sweet and wild celery along the paths, but perhaps most memorable was the abundance of comfrey present in all its many colour forms, blue, magenta, pink, red and white.

WALK 4 HAYSDEN WATER

O.S. MAP SHEET 188

Starting point map reference : 568457

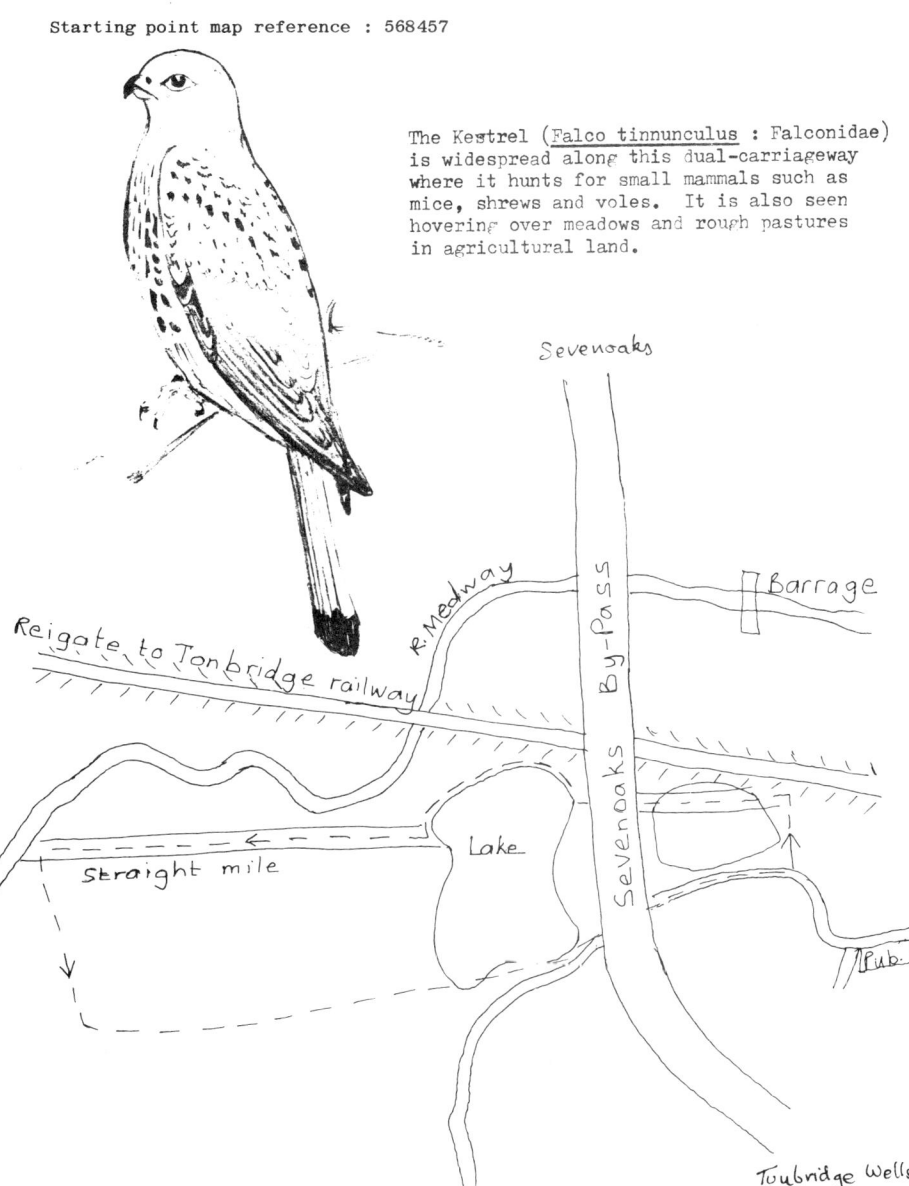

The Kestrel (<u>Falco tinnunculus</u> : Falconidae) is widespread along this dual-carriageway where it hunts for small mammals such as mice, shrews and voles. It is also seen hovering over meadows and rough pastures in agricultural land.

WALK 5   HORSE EYE LEVEL, PEVENSEY

This is a circular bridlepath walk in the middle of Horse Eye Levels which seems to go nowhere; either it is part of some passage to Hailsham or it encloses the only high ground around the farm of Horse Eye. All of the area was presumably under water or very wet in Saxon times. On the map the red bridlepath lines are easily discernable in the expanses of the Levels.

This is a delightful but long walk over the Levels which takes at least 2½ hours at a naturalist's pace. It could be very wet and muddy as it is in a very exposed position with little shelter.

One is left with the impression that much of the bridlepath had been a wide track flanked by hawthorn hedges; much of the hawthorns have disappeared now but those that were present were cascading with white blossom and on this evening meeting the scent was overpowering. The bridlepath appeared to be an agricultural route through low-lying ground and so there are water-filled ditches running on each side of the path for most of the length. The path runs as if it is going straight to Hailsham whose church tower is silhouetted against the horizon and it is probable that the bridlepath links up in some way with the string routes of that noted town. There are footpaths which carry on into Hailsham and in fact one could walk from Hailsham to Horse Eye quite conveniently.

There were a lot of surprising things to see, yellow flags were just coming out, ragged robin was present in one patch only, damsel flies were resting on the reeds, the large brown and blue caterpillars of the lappet moths were feeding avidly on the green reed shoots throughout the length of the path, mute swans were paddling about either in pairs or singly along the many dykes, mallards and the occasional coot were present as well, a few grey herons were out searching for food, hares were seen in groups or singly grazing in the surrounding meadowland, cuckoos could be heard and seen flying from trees and bushes and marsh frogs were disturbed jumping and plopping into the waters. Swifts were with us most of the time collecting up the insects we disturbed whilst walking. Reed warblers chattered away in the reed beds and occasionally we saw them darting away without any chance of seeing them at close quarters.

One of our chance encounters was sighting a black mink which faced us from its secure bolt hole under a bridge. It quickly disappeared back into its labyrinth of tunnels. These animals introduced from America were originally brought over here for the fur trade in 1952.

Most of the walk is easy going on flat or dredged material from the dykes. There is only one part which causes some consternation as it passes down a thin lane overhung with hawthorn and under foot it is well poched up with the trample of bullocks feet. By the White Dyke Farm through which you have to pass the bridlepath widens into an extraordinary 80 foot width - the widest of all bridlepaths ever seen.

WALK 5 HORSE EYE LEVEL, PEVENSEY

O.S. MAP SHEET 199

Starting point map reference : 629087

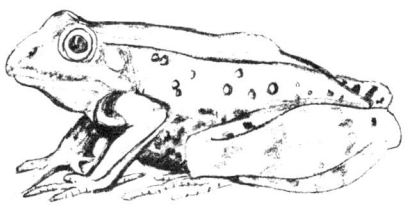

Common Frog (<u>Rana temporaria</u> : Ranidae) - is no longer 'common' in the countryside although it is thriving well in urban areas where there is an abundance of ponds.

WALK 6 JEVINGTON

This is a delightful walk up and along the South Downs past a National Nature Reserve and through Forestry Commission plantations. It is necessary to leave cars in the small village car park on the south side of the village and to start from the church. The different types of habitats that can be appreciated are hedgerows, chalk grassland, scrub, agricultural land and woodland rides.

Much elm had been killed along the bridlepath which leads up from the church. Although we did not attempt a hedge dating we were able to identify eleven species of tree throughout the trip; these included elm, elder, ash, blackthorn, field maple, hawthorn, horse chestnut, hazel, guelder rose, a <u>Prunus</u> species, whitebeam and wild rose.

Those flowers which were out or nearly out on this late day of March included lesser celandine, daisy, speedwells, dogs mercury, dandelion, crocus, carline thistle, dog violets, sweet violets, moschatel and surprisingly some ramsons or wild garlic. Normally these smelly plants are found on the clay soils of the Weald. Wild flowers which were yet to come in flower were cranesbill, cow parsley, figwort, ground ivy, goosegrass, lords and ladies, mullein and escaped raspberry. Harts tongue ferns were present in the hedgerow. One interesting find was the bloody-nosed beetle so called because when you pick it up or disturb this black beetle it exudes a defensive orange red liquid from its mouth.

The bridlepath passes to the north side of the nature reserve, entry to which must be approved from the Nature Conservancy Council (Lewes), up to Winchester's Pond and then southwards through Forestry Commission plantations of softwoods. On the gorse bushes one can see and listen to the characteristic sound of the yellowhammer or listen to the sounds of larks high above. Parts of the nature reserve are enclosed to keep the grazing ponies within. The Forestry Commission (F.C.) rides are not as interesting as along the main South Downs Way but magpies, chaffinches, corn buntings, robins and tits are present. It was very unfortunate to find a fine example of a tawny owl face down and drowned in one of those open water containers the F.C. have for emergency fire control. It was a pity that mesh was not over the top as in other F.C. areas.

WALK 6 JEVINGTON

O.S. MAP SHEET 199

Starting point map reference 563014

The Common Spotted orchid (<u>Dactylorhiza fuchsii</u> : Orchidaceae) is one of the widespread orchids found throughout Sussex and Kent.

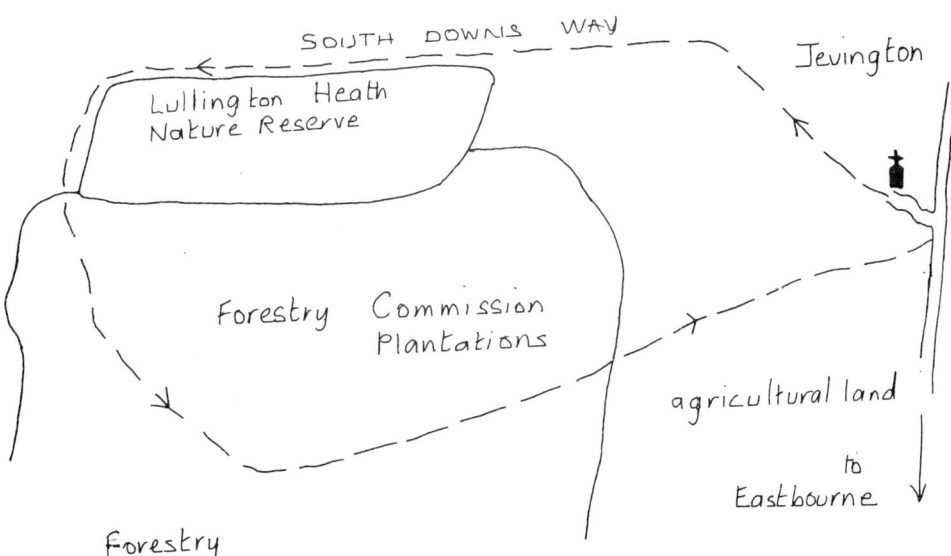

WALK 7   PENHURST, CATSFIELD

This is a circular two mile walk along roads and a very wet bridlepath. Parking is advisable near the delightful rural church of Penhurst close to the pond which often harbours muscovy ducks.

At the stream which leads down from Ashburnham Furnace you can take the bridlepath along a partially made-up road which is lined with hornbeam and hazel. The wild flowers are quite rich along here with common spotted orchids by the Beech Estate boundary. The fields left for hay were sporting quite a variety of flowering plants including moon daisies, bugle, buttercups, vetches and chickweed, while the margin of the bridlepath had some yellow rattle (not very common), salad burnet and pignuts. We watched someone at distance who was only picking moon daisies.

The bridlepath passes through light woods where bluebells, yellow archangel and pignuts grew close to the ford; past a dried up hammer pond now a marshy meadow overgrown at the edges with oak, goat willow and hornbeam.

The going from now on is very wet and muddy, especially below one farm where the bridlepath seemed to be used as a permanent slurry-run for the resident herd. Brooklime was growing in profusion in some of the open water. The bridlepath climbs up through much undergrowth, past some small quarry workings where we saw an abundance of ferns and heard the cuckoo. In another wood there were many ponds which indicated previous iron workings in the area.

Towards the end of the bridlepath the adjacent hedgerow has been completely eliminated and it was necessary to walk straight across a ploughed field and another grazed one, returning to the church via the road. Despite the wet this was a delightful walk.

WALK 7 PENHURST, CATSFIELD

O.S. MAP SHEET 199

Starting point map reference : 688161

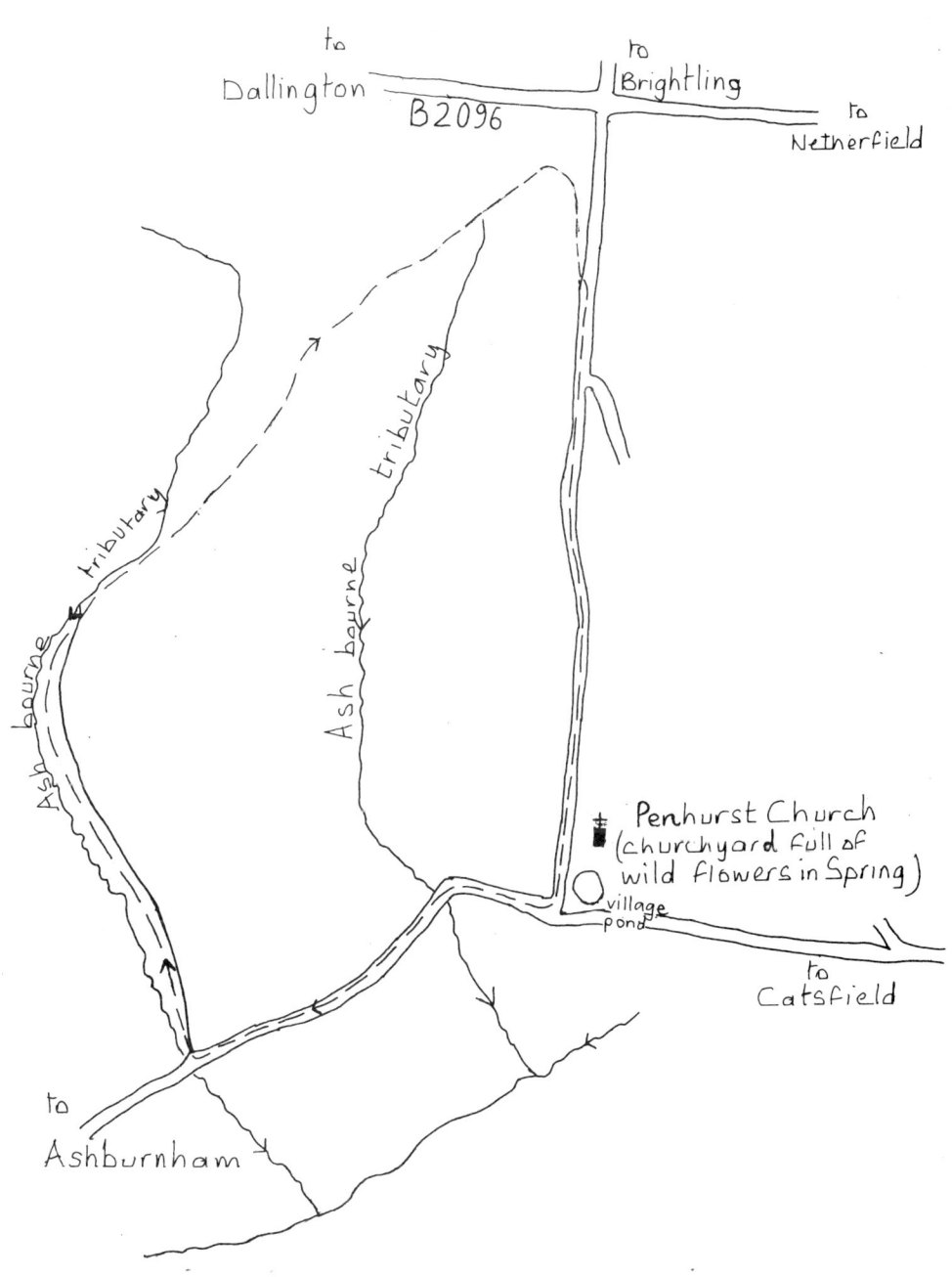

WALK 8   SWIFE TO PUNNETT'S TOWN

        This is an interesting one-way walk which crosses the valley
of the river Dudwell east of Heathfield. The entrance to the bridlepath from the A265 road is wide and quickly drops down from the
houses and scattered plantations of scots pine. There are 300
year old oaks along the western side of the route and an old meadow
which was completely full of mole hills - quite an extraordinary
number (apparently a lot of molehills indicates few moles) - past
an area of coppice and a very neglected area of coppice with
standards, some of the oaks being 400 years old. There were few
birds about but we had a quick glance of a greater spotted woodpecker
- an indicator of ancient woodland - and of a jay.

        The path descends through secondary woods and along a
field with hawthorn scrub and abruptly out into an arable field
where traces of the continuing bridlepath line could be seen. We
descended steeply into hornbeam coppice woodland and down to the
small river Dudwell which exhibited unexpected meandering and
plenty of dark rocks in the water, probably stained from iron
deposits. The ascent on the other side of the valley passes through
fairly open coppice woodland and out onto a vast cleared area where
everything has been bulldozed away - hedges, copses and woods alike.
There were however some neglected corners which supported self heal,
hogweeds, rushes and,surprisingly, some old heads of the burnt tip
orchid which were poking above the remains of snow which had fallen
the previous week. The hill carries on through chestnut coppice
woods with a distinct ground layer of hard ferns.

        In the open area there are fine views over the surrounding
countryside which showed at this early time of the year the colour
changes in the different types of woods, with their leaf buds
swelling up: the browns of the hornbeam, the white of the oaks
and the orange of the willows. Near the top a small stream supports
a very good example of alder along its length (an alder carr).

        The bridlepath eventually comes out on a small minor road
and here we dated the hedge; two thirty-yard sections had 7 and 8
species giving an average figure of 750 years; this is therefore
probably a thirteenth-century hedgerow which today looks
undistinguished; being cut back on top of a substantial bank -
the raised bank itself being a good sign of longevity.

        There were quite a few birds recorded on this winter's day,
10 magpies were seen together (they typically aggregate in winter),
wood pigeon, chaffinch, crow, blue tit, nuthatch, common gull,
blackbird, skylark, kestrel, lapwing, house sparrow, robin and wren.

WALK 8   SWIFE TO PUNNETT'S TOWN

O.S. MAP SHEET 199

Starting point map reference : 621229

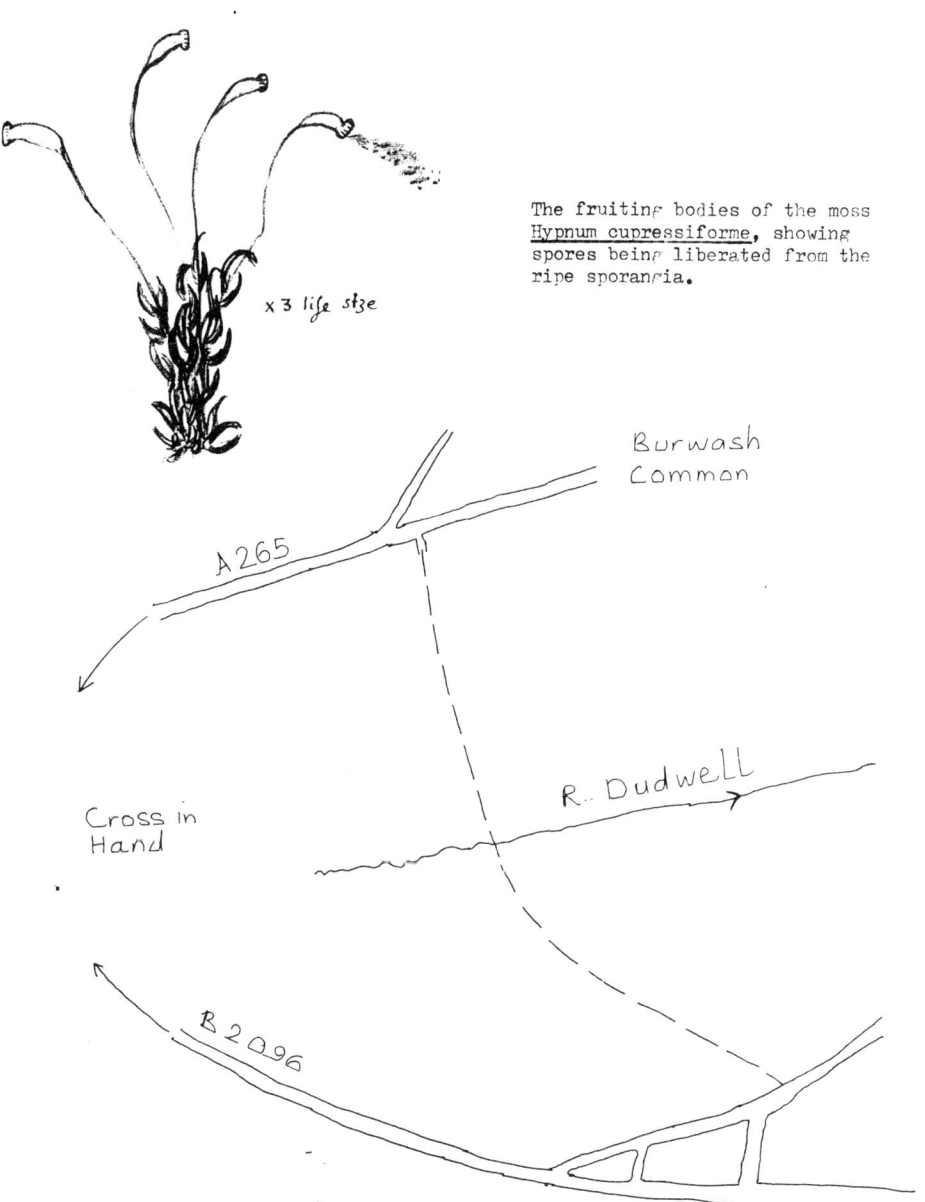

The fruiting bodies of the moss <u>Hypnum cupressiforme</u>, showing spores being liberated from the ripe sporangia.

WALK 9   IDEN WOOD, RYE FOREIGN

This walk comprises bridlepath and footpath through coppice woodlands and farmland. It can be exceedingly muddy particularly after rain and on this March morning it was especially so; nevertheless we found the wealth of wildlife so encouraging that we enjoyed the walk enormously.

We met whilst it was still raining after overnight rain and storms and it was still very blustery. It would have been nice to set off along the wide and very typical bridlepath but it was far too muddy to attempt, instead we moved off through sweet chestnut coppice, through a woodman's yard and followed parallel with the bridlepath.

The bridlepath bank was impressive. It was at least two metres high and for the most part had neglected hornbeam coppiced trees along its length representing a time when this species was used more efficiently as a layered hedgerow. The bank was completely covered in mosses, very impressive at this time of the year when many of them are sporting their reproductive bodies called sporangia - and all of a verdant green colour which can be very distinctive on a rainy day. There were also groups of the hard fern and a variety of grey coloured lichens on the banks. In the adjacent coppices the mosses and lichens were at their best around the bases of the oak standard trees and round the bases of the chestnut stools. Here and there the bright green mantle had been scratched out by rabbits of which there were plenty of tell-tale signs. The bridlepath bank had made superb opportunities for rabbit warrens particularly where it was overgrown, and there were signs that a badger sett was present; we almost stepped into a badger latrine.

In the coppice woodland there were extensive patches of honeysuckle, some wood sage sprouting up, coral spot fungus in the dead trees, and pestle puffballs on the fallen timber. This is the only British puffball which grows out of wood and it is edible. The very variable and colourful fungus Tagetes versicolor was present on some stumps. The wild flowers which we saw but which were not in flower were the bluebell, lesser celandine, mullein, and along the road alexanders which is a coast-loving plant. Birds which we saw included the dunnock, chaffinch, carrion crow, fieldfare, blackbird, mistle thrush, wren and great tit.

The walk passes close to an estate on the western boundary, passes through the middle of Old House Farm and then back through woods and orchards.

WALK 9   IDEN WOOD, RYE FOREIGN

O.S. MAP SHEET 189

Starting point map reference : 903231

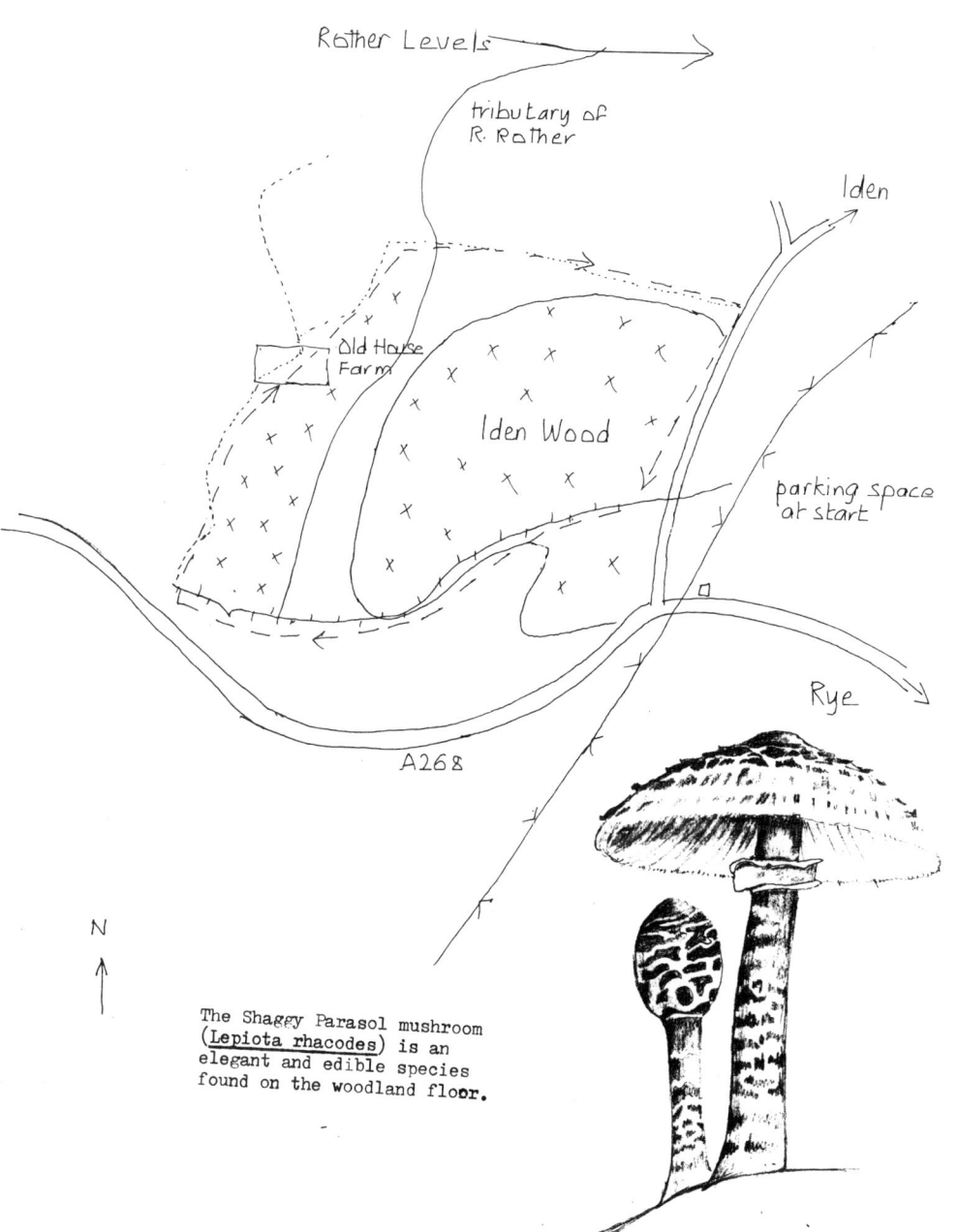

The Shaggy Parasol mushroom (<u>Lepiota rhacodes</u>) is an elegant and edible species found on the woodland floor.

WALK 10   THE RIDGE, TO COGHURST, HASTINGS

This is another one-way downhill walk so it is necessary to leave some transport at the other end of the road near Coghurst Caravan Park.

This turned out to be another fascinating and typical bridlepath walk steeped in antiquity. We set off from Beaney Lane down a wide rough road lined on either side by the bridlepath hedges. We soon carried out a hedge-dating which gave us the following results:

Woody Species	sample 1	sample 2	sample 3
Spindle	+	–	–
Oak species	+	+	+
Field Maple	+	+	+
Sloe	+	+	+
Rose	+	+	+
Hazel	+	+	+
Hornbeam	+	–	+
Hawthorn	+	+	+
Ash	–	+	–
Total species	8	7	7

There was also holly and goat willow about so that eleven species were seen in about 100 metres of hedgerow.

The bridlepath progressed downhill as a fine example of a sunken lane which has a path which follows it on the drier high banks, first on one side and then on the other. The path is still used by horseriders as we met one and looks as though it would be a very muddy path to walk in wet weather. On the west of the path there is a Maplehurst Wood which is designated as a Site of Special Scientific Interest. (S.S.S.I.)

We were soon enchanted with a nightingale in full song which sang strongly with no reservation or objection to our close proximity although we never saw him. It was we who left him singing. At our feet were a few tall spikes of early purple orchids and there was quite a lot of Town Hall Clock (Moschatel) that delightful plant which has a square flower which resembles a clock face, with one on the top. Other woodland flowers included greater stitchworts, bugles, pignuts and figworts (the latter not in flower), bluebells, and yellow archangels along the path which wound along the hedgerows, past a small pond which only seemed to be lacking a kingfisher.

The bridlepath is probably best along the first section from the ridge to the first small lane to Westfield. We crossed this and progressed along the rest of the bridlepath and joined a footpath which took us up past Eastlands Farm - rather out of our way - after we had met the farmer at the end of the lane who advised us that the bridge over the stream towards Coghurst Farm was down.

WALK 10 THE RIDGE TO COGHURST, HASTINGS

O.S. MAP SHEET 199

Starting point map reference : 810127

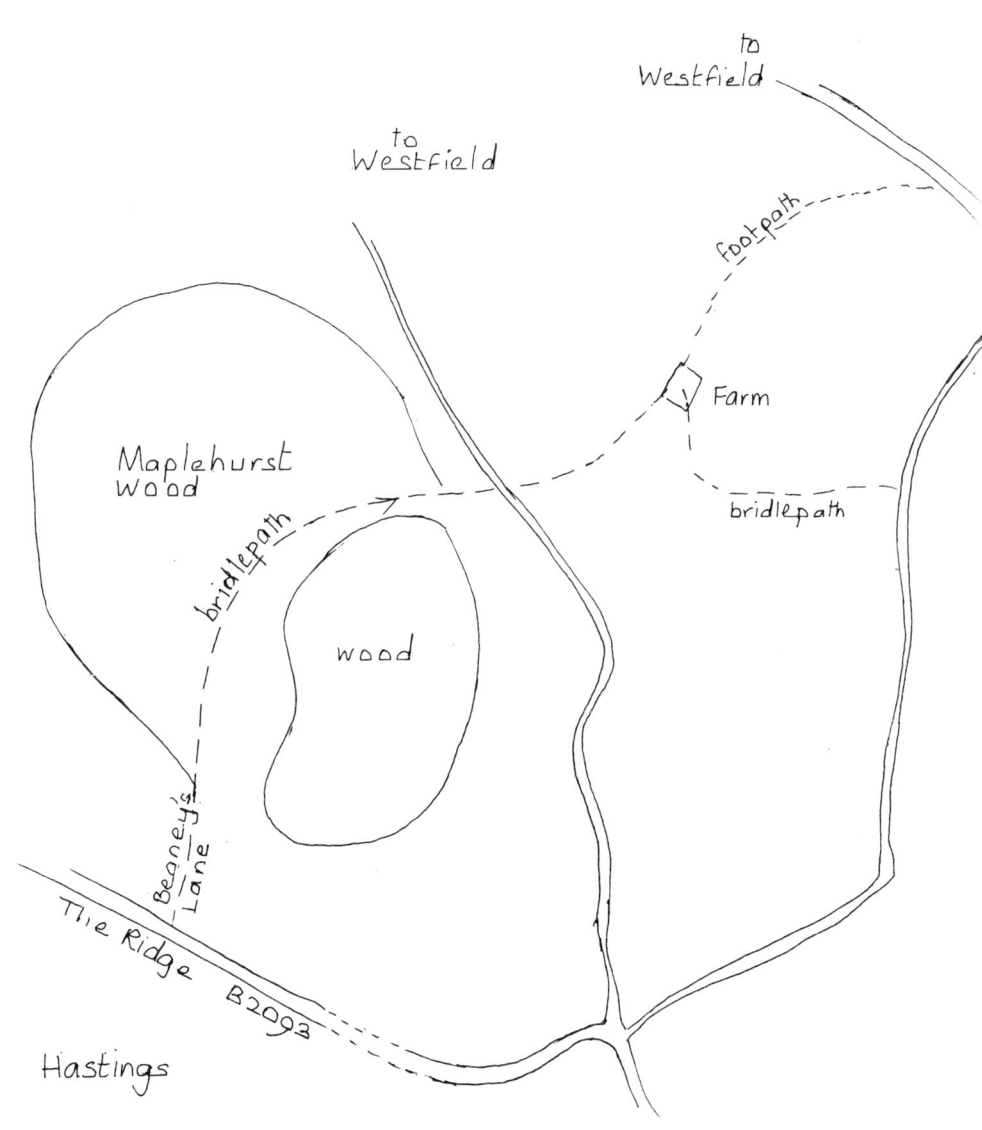

FOOTPATHS

WALKS 11 - 20

WALK 11 ABBOT'S WOOD, POLEGATE

This is a showpiece of the Forestry Commission (F.C.) and worthy of a visit.

It is crossed by a bridlepath and there is the famous Plackett Walk for disabled people (less than ¼ mile long) which was opened in 1979. Ample parking and picnic sites are available as well as a leaflet dispenser.

The woodland is a mixture of scots pine, corsican pine, western hemlock and norway spruce (Christmas Trees!) and with a little detective work it is possible to see what was there before the F.C. moved in - namely, oak woodland, as there are still quite a few standards of about 300 years of age. There is a very large and possibly 400-year old oak along the main route (2 miles) which must have been an acorn when the Mary Rose went down.

Mounds of wood ants abound here in what is probably one of their best sites in S.E. England (cf. Bedgebury). Rabbits, squirrels, badgers and dogs have dug into their strongholds of pine needles which are often seen disturbed close to the paths - where dogs' mercury, an indicator of secondary woodland, and yellow archangel occur with the edible pestle puffballs sticking out of decayed wood. We witnessed a male brimstone butterfly feeding on the nectar of primroses - a good observation as it is this butterfly with its long tongue which is the principal pollinator of primroses. There were plenty of speckled wood butterflies which followed us along the rides. A hornbeam hedgerow gave us some splendid views of contorted trees which had been layered in the past.

On the lake - an ancient stewpond stocked with fish - all was quiet - a pair of Canada geese were nesting; the female sitting on the safe island nest and the male standing its own against visitors on the bank. Mallards were as usual, in abundance. At the end of the walk the path passes through some very pleasant oak woods which have had their softwood protector crop removed and the sight of these 30 year old trees mixed with bluebells, yellow archangels and wood anemones was very pleasing.

WALK 11 ABBOT'S WOOD, POLEGATE

O.S. MAP SHEET 199

Starting point map reference : 557075

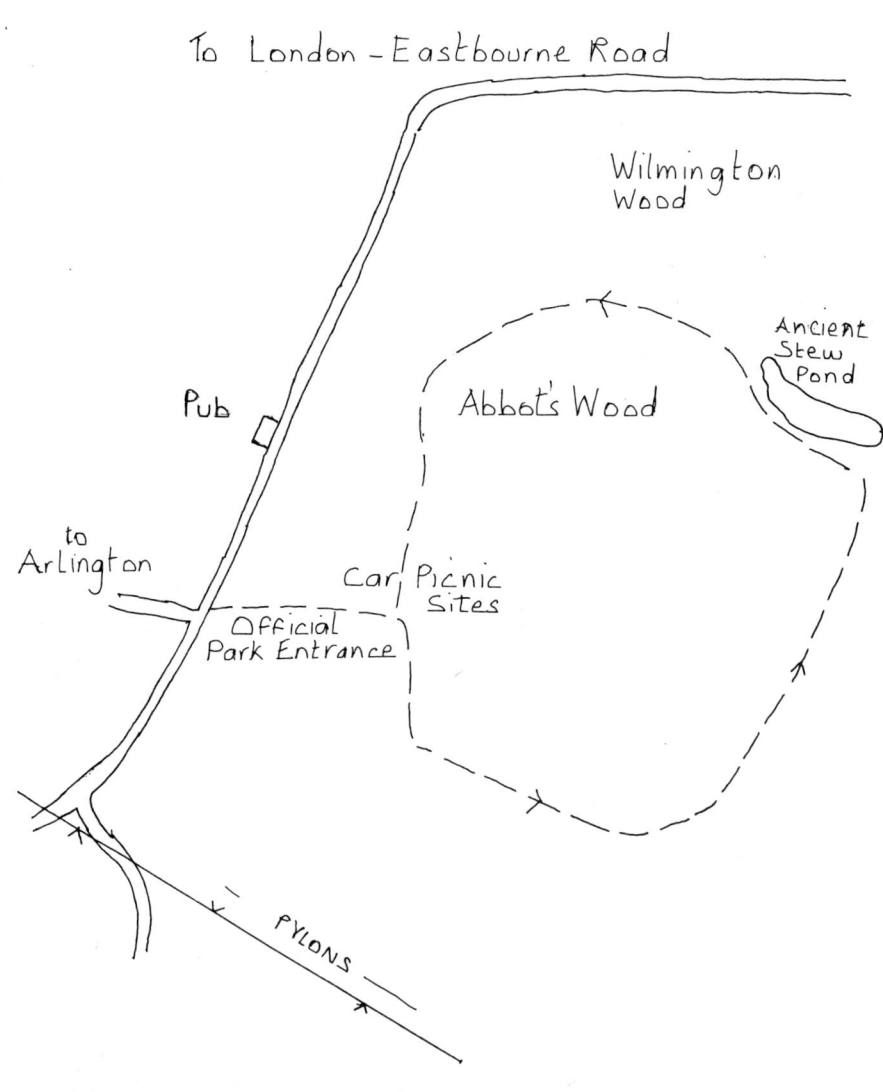

WALK 12 BEACHY HEAD NATURE TRAIL

This is a walk of about $1\frac{1}{4}$ miles which is continuous for the most part with the South Downs Way. Only the latter is marked and entrance downhill is easy to find, although the nature trail starts at the centre where there is an information board. There are 4200 acres or $6\frac{1}{2}$ square miles of land up here, overlooking Eastbourne and belonging to the Eastbourne Borough, on which to study wildlife. It is a great tourist attraction so choose your time carefully, if you want quiet.

The walk follows a gentle undulating path at the top of the cliffs and passes through chalk grassland, varying degrees of scrub and thickets and open downland. There are excellent opportunities for ornithologists - warblers, pipits, wrens, gulls and migrants - and for botanists as the area supports a wealth of chalk-loving vetches, grasses and trees.

Of outstanding interest were the four different colour forms of milkwort which in places formed blue beds in the turf - deep blue, light blue, white and pink. They were mixed with buttercups, small daisies (plants are very much smaller here because of the exposed position and salt spray), cut leaved cranesbill, herb robert and birds foot trefoil. Mignonette was out in places, hemlock was pushing up with its finely divided leaves and red speckled stems and in the undergrowth cleavers and bryony with its shiny leaves were competing for place.

On this morning visit we were greeted by the welcome sound of a single nightingale making incomplete songs in the buckthorn thickets. Chaffinch, willow warblers and wrens and a possible stonechat completed the melodious chattering in the scrub bushes.

Trees and shrub bushes were of interest; the white leaves of whitebeam and the cream flowers of the wayfaring trees were conspicuous by their presence and contrast with the light green privet mixed with wild apple and cherry.

WALK 12   BEACHY HEAD NATURE TRAIL

O.S. MAP SHEET 199

Starting point map reference : 583954

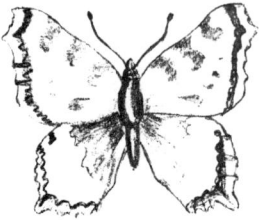

The Small Tortoiseshell butterfly (<u>Aglais urticae</u> : Nymphalidae) is common along hedgerows and in the corner of fields where its larval foodplant the nettle (<u>Urtica dioica</u> : Urticaceae) occurs.

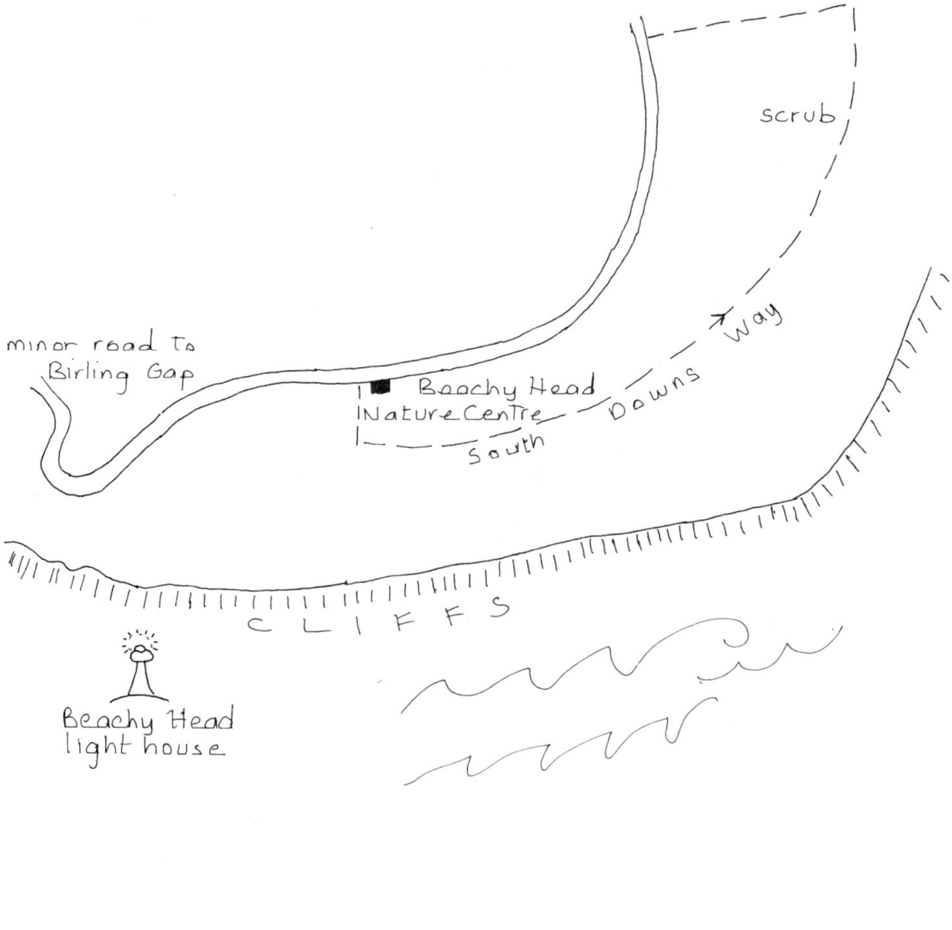

WALK 13 BRIGHTLING

This scenic walk makes use of a footpath, a bridlepath and a minor road and passes by a typical hammer pond, still containing water. The best place to park is at the streambridge where three species of orchid can be found in May; early purple, common spotted and common twayblade. The damp areas by the stream are a riot of wild flowers, wild garlic, yellow archangel, bluebell, figwort, herb robert and an unusual one, coral root bitter cress.

The path goes uphill to two large blue silos (or used to, for the silos were pulled down a few weeks later), and passes through open and mixed woodland with oak, open grassland with thistles, nettles and bugle, past a small farm pond with blanket moss, challock and mallards. The bridlepath comes out onto a minor road at the farm.

Progressing along the road it is then necessary to walk in the entrance to the Gypsum mines and immediately take a footpath off to the left. This is not too easy to find. On the entrance verges early purple orchids were growing. The footpath descends through open fields to a bluebell and wild garlic wood, across a small stream where golden saxifrage covering some of the damp banks and up through some thick undergrowth. Look out for a fox's earth.

The bridlepath is joined again in an open area which had been planted up with conifers; it descends through open fields where a hedgerow has been removed and past a small cottage. Other plants to be seen were primrose, pilewort and pignut. There was an exceptionally large sallow tree growing by the side of a small pond towards the end of the walk.

WALK 13 BRIGHTLING

O.S. MAP SHEET 199

Starting point map reference : 689223

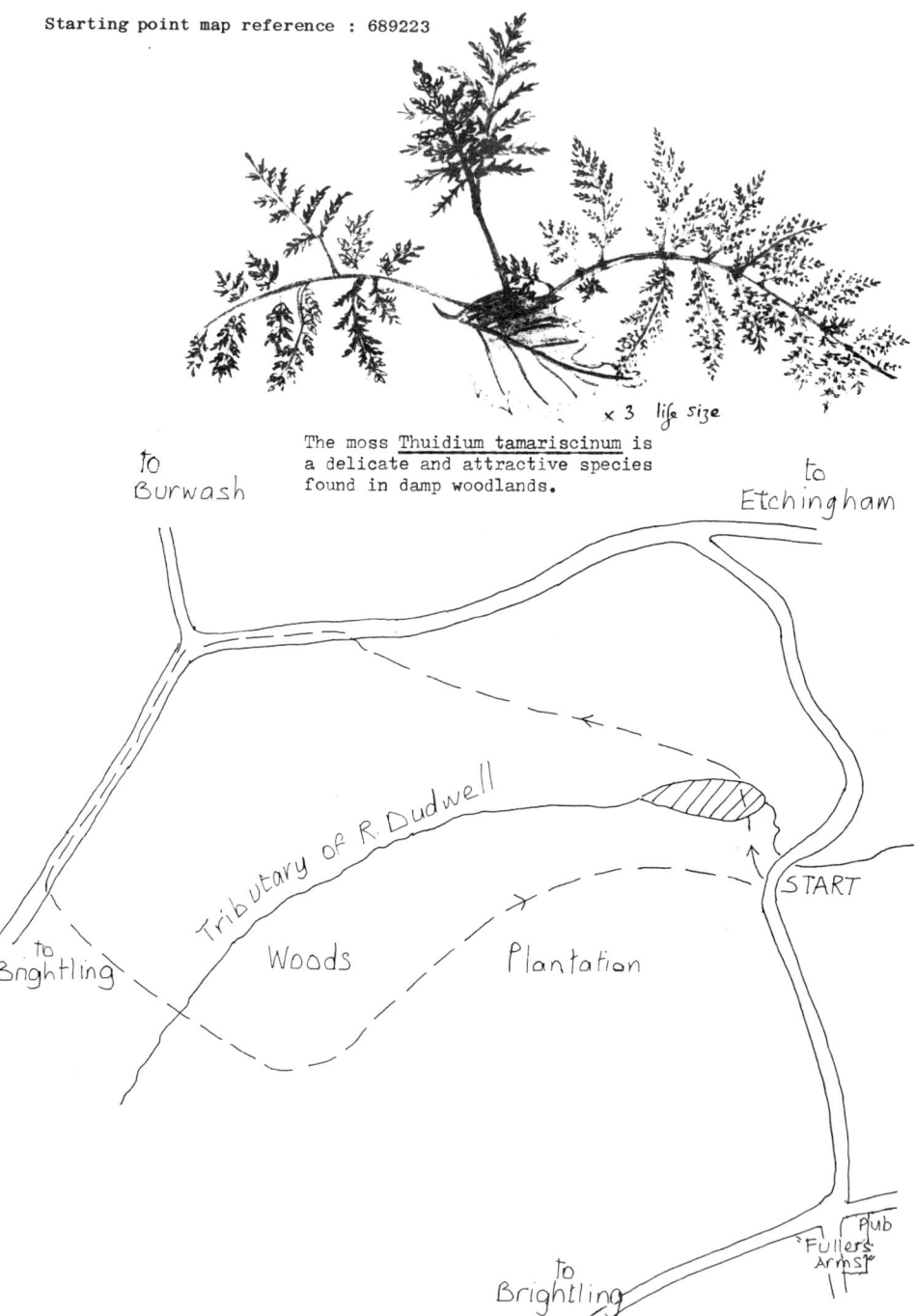

The moss <u>Thuidium tamariscinum</u> is a delicate and attractive species found in damp woodlands.

WALK 14   FOOTLANDS WOOD, BATTLE

      This is an excellently well-laid out F.C. plantation with large car park and explanatory leaflets in a dispenser (5p). The trees were planted in 1936 and are in two main lots - conifers and beech - thus the walk takes in two very different and contrasting habitats. Beechwood whose woodland floor is studded with bluebells as far as the eye can see - and rows of conifers whose rich pile of needles clothe the dark woodland floor denying any form of life for flowering plants - just here and there where shafts of sunlight fall some leaves of bluebell which will never flower or some long-drawn-out leaves of bramble or wood anemone.

      The light beechwood was criss-crossed with badger runs and eventually we came across the tidy sett with about four enormous holes. Thrown out of the setts were many pellets of thick clay and there were quite a lot of bluebell leaves lying about - perhaps part of some summer bedding. Grey squirrels were not seen but there was plenty of evidence of them about.

      There were about twenty species of wild flower in flower including primrose, common dog violet, golden saxifrage (by the stream) and cuckoo flower; the leaflet noted that 140 species had been recorded here in the past. Birds were not really in evidence except near the car park where tame chaffinches and blackbirds clearly thrived on scraps from picnickers. A group of cole tits were seen working the larch buds, siskins were heard calling from the canopy, wood pigeons were heard and not seen clattering away from the tree tops and wrens were heard throughout singing with their characteristic melodious calls.

      In the centre of the wood the small pond only appeared to support pond skaters - the woodland glade in this area looked suitable for the speckled wood butterfly but the weather was a little too cold for butterflies. At least ten different types of tree were seen apart from the Scots and Corsican pine, Japanese larch, western hemlock, Lawsons cyprus and grand fir put in by the F.C., these included oak, sweet chestnut, goat willow and sycamore.

WALK 14 FOOTLANDS WOOD, BATTLE

O.S. MAP SHEET 199

Starting point map reference : 763204

Polytrichium commune, a bristly type of moss found close to woodland streams.

x 3 life size

Barnes Wood

Vinehall

to Cripp's Corner

Footlands Wood

tributary of R. Brede

to Whatlington

WALK 15 FOREST WAY, HARTFIELD

Disused railway lines open to the public lend themselves ideally to walks in the countryside, because they are flat, without obstacles and become overgrown with wild flowers, shrubs and trees. Once onto the old tracks disabled naturalists in wheelchairs would find the going relatively easy. This East Grinstead to Tunbridge Wells line was axed by Dr. Beeching in the 1960's and therefore gives us an insight into fifteen years of uncontrolled growth along the line.

Two Centre for Continuing Education classes tackled two different sections of this line on consecutive days, westbound from Hartfield station and westwards from the bridge over the B2110 road between Hartfield and Groombridge. Both were made into circular walks by returning on the north side of the line by footpaths.

Certain plants were in abundance along the track - comfrey (once called knitbone as it was used to help broken bones) was present as large leaved clumps, meadow sweet sometimes occupied complete ground cover for several metres and marsh marigolds were on the watery margins of the track. Cowslips and primroses were not very common but common twayblades and common spotted orchids were present by the thousand.

The footpath returns on the other side of the Medway stream which meanders through the valley. We were surprised to find that the path was obstructed by a large deer farm which pressed us close to the stream. Heron and Canada geese were present, the latter were actually nesting. Cuckoos and willow warblers were heard throughout the walk.

WALK 15 FOREST WAY, HARTFIELD

O.S. MAP SHEET 188

Starting point map reference : 479362

The Lapwing or Peewit (<u>Vanellus vanellus</u> : Charadriidae) is an autumn migrant and upwards of several thousand can be seen in some large fields in the weald where they search for worms and other invertebrates.

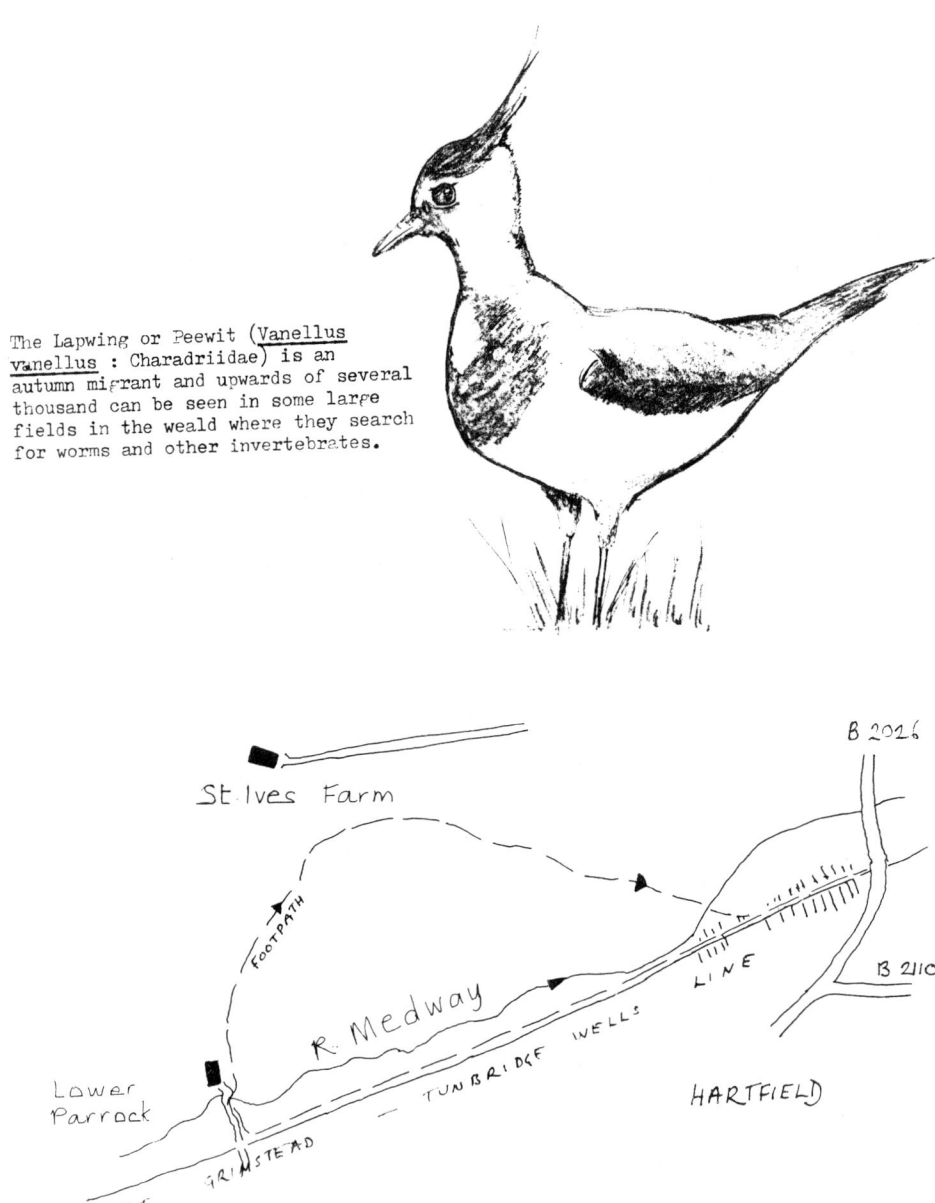

WALK 16 GREAT WOOD, BATTLE

   This is a F.C. plantation of mixed species on sand and clay as witnessed by the abundance of silver birch. At the beginning of the walk there is a small plantation of Norway Spruce and deciduous trees including elm and poplar as well as some evergreen eucalyptus trees present. One solitary specimen of snake bark maple is close to the first division of the road. The habitats of interest to naturalists include the wide rides and small meadows at intersections.

   Botanically, the rides, which are quite wide, are very rich; in a few places the grass was pink with the mat-like growths of lousewort mixed in with a little blue milkwort. This latter species was present in at least two colour varieties, white and blue, but it does not grow as well as at Beachy Head Nature Trail. Common spotted orchids have been established in very sizeable colonies in some places at the edge of the rides - up to sixty rosettes of very spotted leaves were present in one small colony of three square yards - a few just shooting up with spikes.

   Other wild flowers present were spring cinquefoil, silverweed (leaves only) bugle which was often very tall and in thick clumps, yellow pimpernel, greater stitchwort, wood sage, red campion, bluebell and less often herb robert, heather, bedstraws, Sphagnum mosses and hard ferns. Early spring flowers were on their way out such as wood anemone, primrose and violets and later flowering summer flowers were on their way up including rose bay willow herb, nettle and knapweeds.

   Our surprise was a vixen fox in sultry colours which appeared along one of the rides and peered at us with similar curiosity. There are plenty of rabbits about which probably support the fox population. In the trees were plenty of wrens, chiffchaffs, thrushes, blackbirds and magpies. Day-flying speckled yellow moths were conspicuous by their presence and followed us about, whilst up on the tips of the trees we could see the aggregations of the small long-horned moths which were swirling about.

WALK 16 GREAT WOOD, BATTLE

O.S. MAP SHEET 199

Starting point map reference : 765164

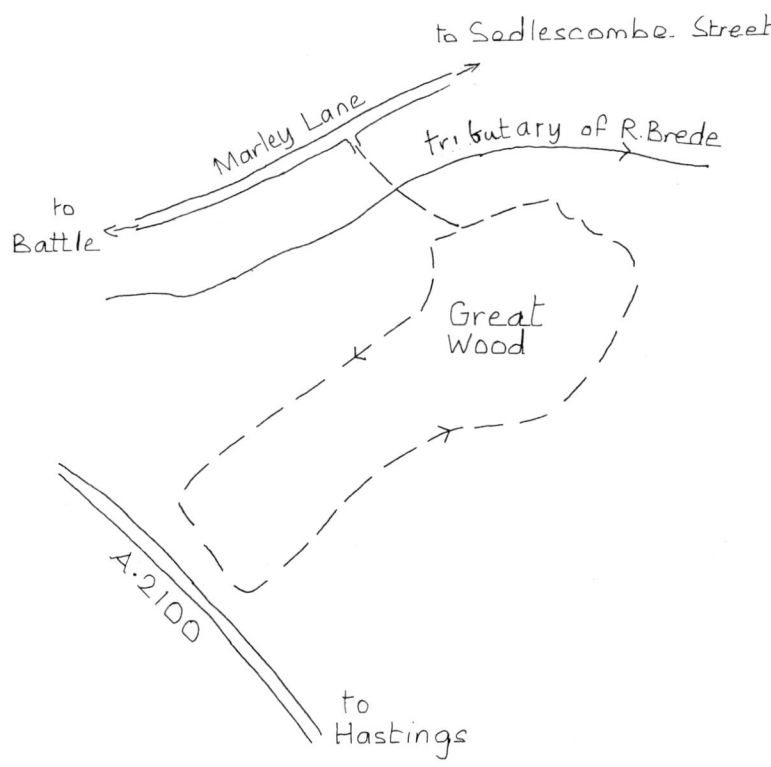

WALK 17   OCTAVIA HILL WOODLAND

There is a modest entrance charge for cars for these woodlands that had their name changed from Toys Hill woodlands in 1981 to commemorate for ever the good work of Octavia Hill in setting up the National Trust. There are no toilet facilities, no information kiosk and no facilities for the disabled, though it is very popular. Around the car park to the east there are extensive open beech woods with little undergrowth. All the walks are marked with blue plastic arrows.

Walking north-east however one can follow an old driveway lined with rhododendrons and laurel; this progresses into mixed woodland with oak and birch and some old pollarded beech and oak. Little plant variety was encountered. Some wood sorrel was present as well as honeysuckle and a cuckoo was heard. The path then goes downhill and the wild flowers increase dramatically; eventually the road comes out at the Tally Ho pub.

Altogether some 42 wild flower species were recorded (not all in flower) as well as ten species of tree and shrub and 13 species of bird.

Along the road to the Octavia Hill well there are fine views over the Weald to Hever and Four Elms. The cars can be rejoined by walking up the road through the steep Scords wood where holly occurs as an understorey below beech.

Octavia Hill's modest gravestone is under an ancient yew at the entrance to the Crockham Hill church graveyard. She was buried there with her sister in 1930. The churchyard was alive with primroses everywhere and the woodland behind was full of bluebells and red campion.

WALK 17 OCTAVIA HILL WOODLAND

O.S. MAP SHEET 188

Starting point map reference : 470516

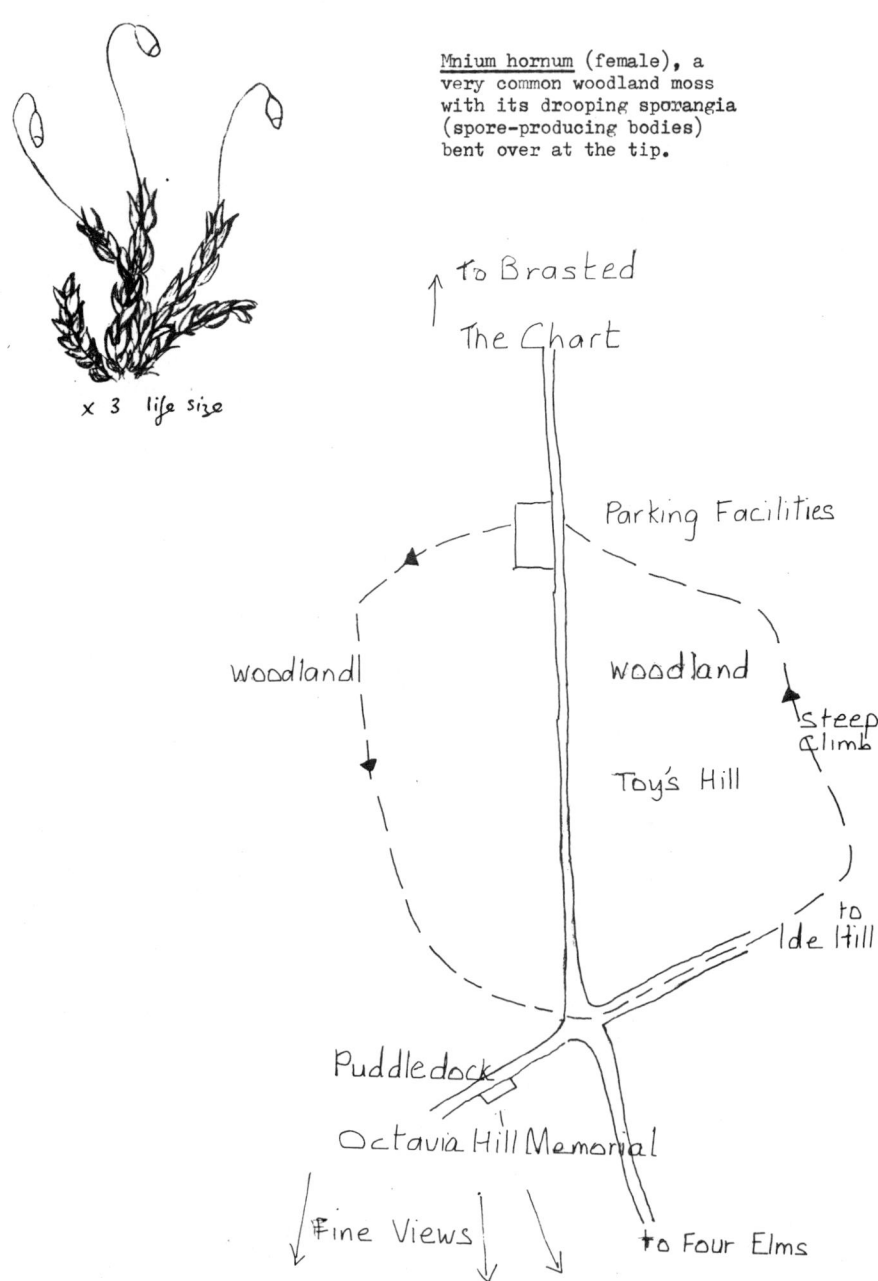

Mnium hornum (female), a very common woodland moss with its drooping sporangia (spore-producing bodies) bent over at the tip.

x 3 life size

WALK 18 RUSHLAKE GREEN

This is an excellent route for those who cannot manage too strenuous a walk. No stiles, barbed wire or fences, with scenic views over the South Downs. The first half of the route follows a tarmac road which is the footpath up to the Priory, now a restaurant.

The footpath is banked by terrific amounts of wild flowers benefitting by not being along major roads; these included dog violets, wood anemones (still out), wood sorrel (over), bluebells, bugle, yellow archangel, herb robert, stitchworts, primroses (still out), silverweed (not yet out) and one common spotted orchid with unopened flower spike.

At the Priory the footpath joins the bridlepath and here it is necessary to turn right. The grass bridlepath is typically a wide one with hedgerows on each side, the banks supporting figworts, thistles, red campion and stitchworts. The path becomes a little boggy where you must bear right up a loggers' track through oakwoods. Look out for speckled wood butterflies along the rides and in the glades. It opens into an arable field where one has to walk along the hedgerow and up onto a sandy ridge where some cottages occur. Here the broom was well in flower and doing well on the sandy soil.

The trees up the sandy track are chestnut, hawthorn and oak, holly, sycamore and field maple. There are plenty of lords and ladies along the roadside which you follow to return to the start.

WALK 18 RUSHLAKE GREEN

O.S. MAP SHEET 199

Starting point map reference : 640192

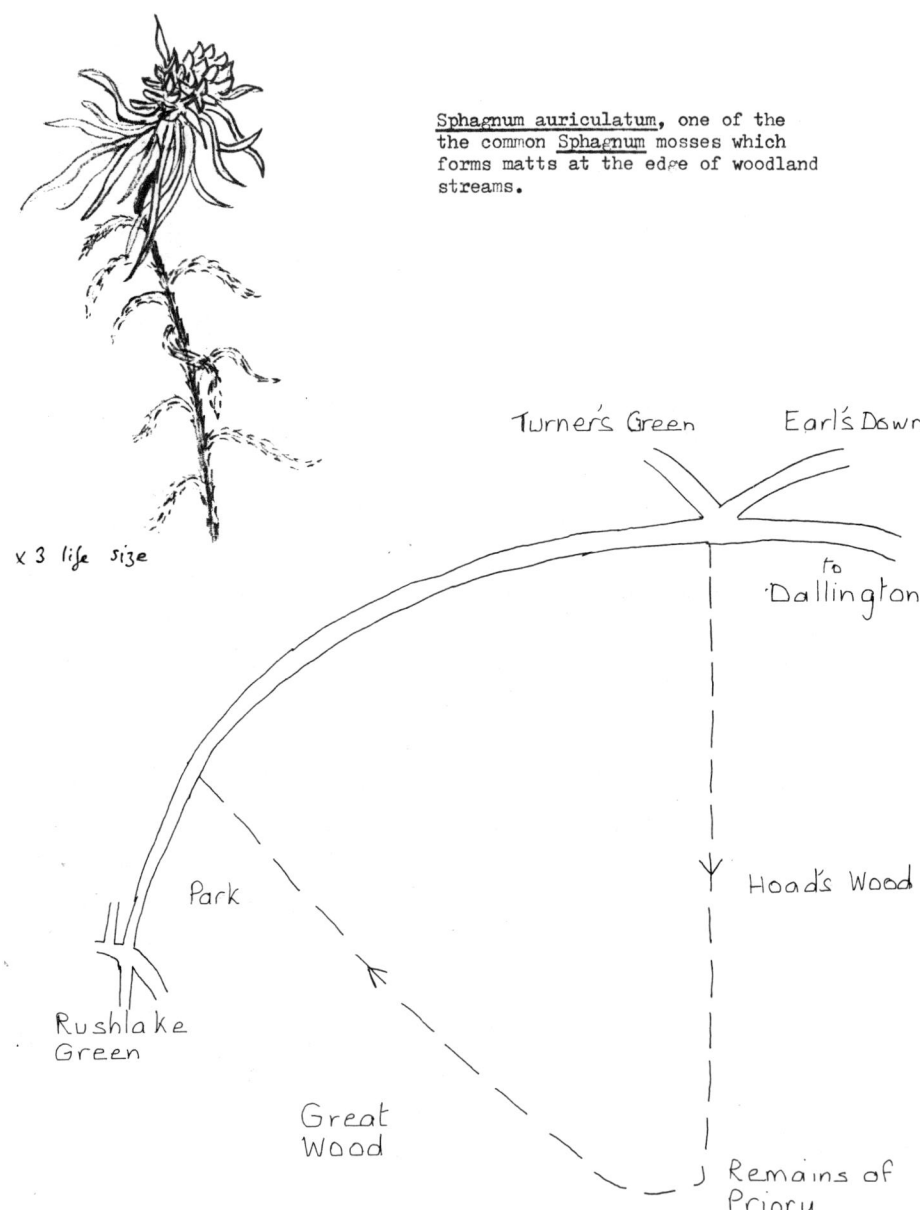

Sphagnum auriculatum, one of the the common Sphagnum mosses which forms matts at the edge of woodland streams.

x 3 life size

WALK 19   CUCKMERE AND SEAFORD HEAD

This is a long and picturesque walk which can be accomplished in 2½ hours as a round trip from the Seven Sisters Country Park. Alternatively, one can drive through the housing estate to the west of Chyngton Farm and up onto South Hill car park which is always open. During 1982 we did both of these walks.

The habitats available to naturalists are water meadows, freshwater and estuarine sites, chalk grassland and scrub. One surprising observation we made with the Battle group was a solitary spoonbill which was resting in the meadows between the Cuckmere meanders. This was a very fortunate observation for spoonbills are only recorded two or three times in the south-east each year, and this specimen was probably off course from its summer residence on the continent. Herons, mute swans, lapwings and black headed gulls are often seen down here on the levels.

The path from Exceat Bridge passes through a pub car park and along old hedgerows. As the path climbs certain areas of steep unploughed pasture sport examples of meadow clary - a very infrequently-met wild flower. The path eventually comes out at some cottages which overlook the estuary. Here it is necessary to climb up towards the west and up to that part of the Seaford Head Nature reserve which is dominated by chalk grassland sward, thick scrub and cliffs. One can deviate into this part of the reserve to Hope Gap or continue straight up to car park at South Hill. If parking at South Hill a round trip on the reserve can be had by walking up to the golf course, down a hollow to Hope Gap and back up one of the gentle slopes in the Downs to the car.

At South Hill marvellous views over the Friston area can be had, particularly over the Friston Forest plantations behind the Seven Sisters Country Park Centre and over the Seven Sisters cliffs which looks out over the Channel. The return walk descends down the concrete road to Chyngton Farm with good views over Seaford where on one of the evening walks a terrific noise of singing blackbirds in everyone's garden was quite distinctive over the quiet Downs. After the farm the footpath branches to the east and makes its way through various fields to the Exceat Bridge once more.

WALK 19 CUCKMERE AND SEAFORD HEAD

O.S. MAP SHEET 199

Starting point map reference : 518994

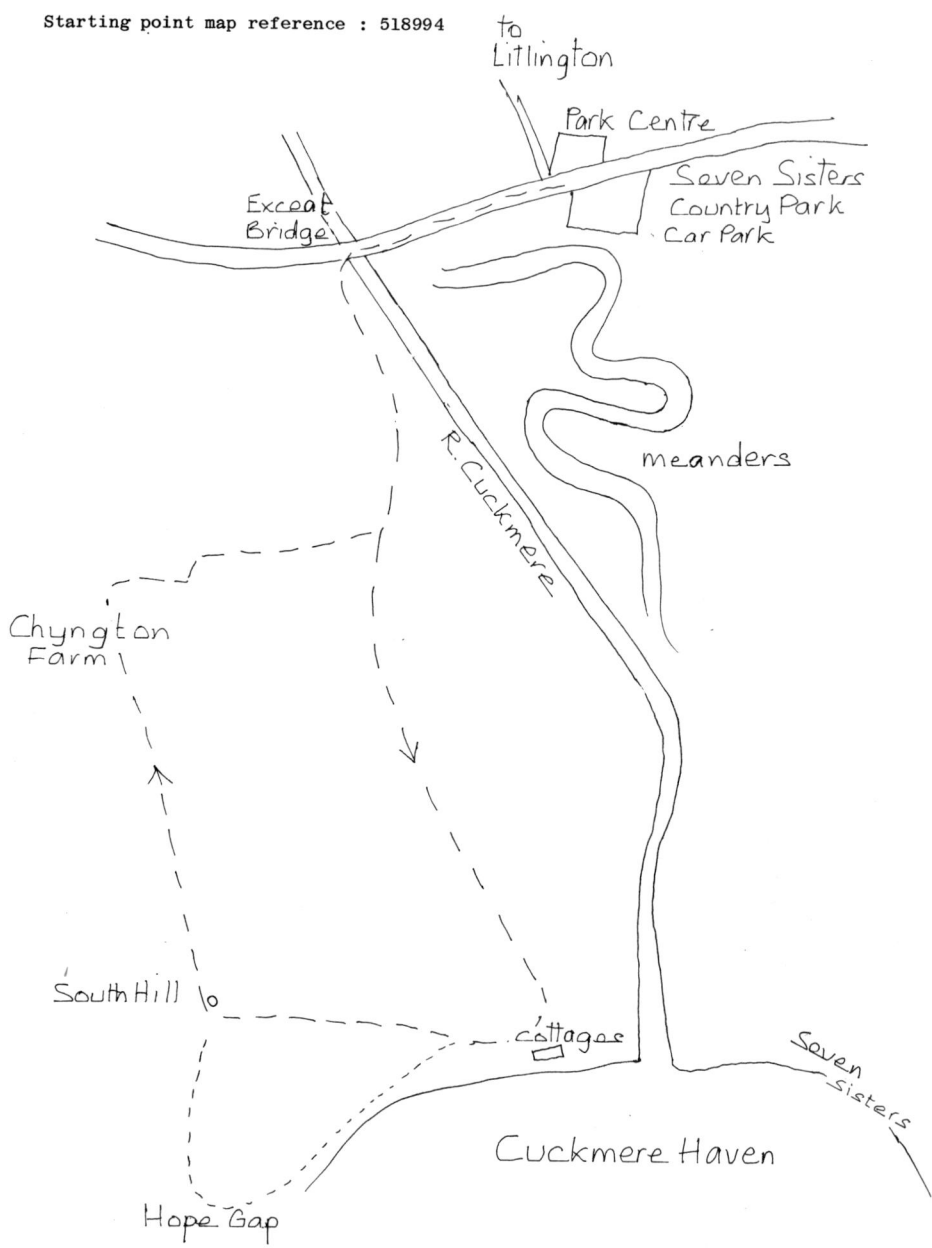

WALK 20   500 ACRE WOOD, ASHDOWN FOREST

The walk starts close to the Half Moon public house and passes up the drive towards a large house and estate. There are plantations on the right and much activity from badgers; their regular paths and slippery slides down the banks being very obvious. There are some splendid pollarded oaks with spreading canopies which must be in excess of 500 years of age and predate the age of the house at the end of the drive.

The footpath veers to the left and eventually comes out at a large artificial pond much frequented by fishermen. There are large pollarded beech trees around and much felling of chestnut coppice had been done.

There are several different paths to take and get lost in but eventually you must choose one large one that goes to the left. There are remnants of what vegetations used to be here before the whole area was put down to conifers - large pollarded beeches and yews. The open coppiced areas are interesting to walk through, with wood sage and willowherbs sprouting up.

The last part of the walk is on the typical Ashdown Forest scenery with bracken and silver birch. There had been some ancient excavations on this part of the forest as witnessed by the numerous mounds and pits throughout.

WALK 20 500 ACRE WOOD, ASHDOWN FOREST

O.S. MAP SHEET 188

Starting point map reference : 496332

Mnium hornum (male) with clusters of rosettes.

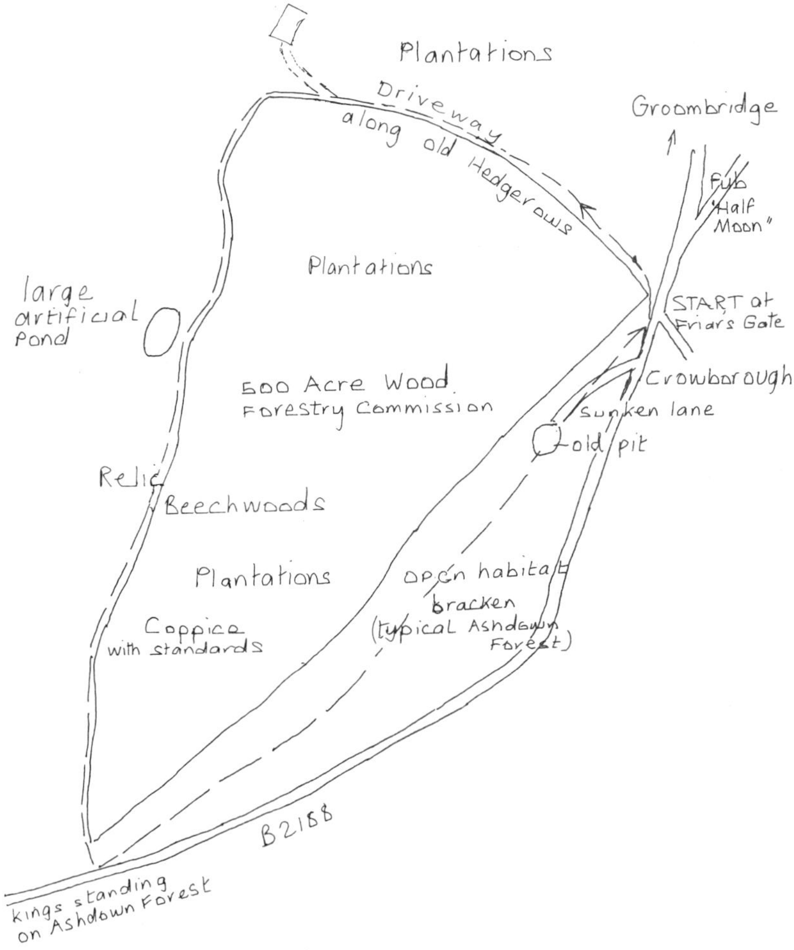

× 3 life size

BIBLIOGRAPHY

Armstrong, J.R. 1978. A History of Sussex. Phillimore & Co. Ltd., London and Chichester.

Buckley, S.E., 1948, Rural rides by William Cobbett. Harrap & Co. Ltd., London.

Feltwell, J.S.E., 1982. Field Trips with Adults - their practicalities and potential for the science class. Tutors' Bull. 5 (1) 10-11.

Horwood, A.R., 1919. A new British Flora, British Wild Flowers,. Gresham Publishing Co. Ltd., London.

Pollard, E., Hooper, M.D. and Moore, N.W., 1974. Hedges. Collins, London, New Naturalist Series.

Streeter, D. and Richardson, R. 1982. Discovering Hedgerows. BBC Publications.

Thomas, E. & White, J.T., 1980. Hedgerows, Ash & Grant, London

Wildlife and Countryside Act., 1981. H.M.S.O., London. Part III Public Rights of Way.

USEFUL ADDRESSES

Forestry Commission,
Chief Forester,
Forest Office,
NETHERFIELD,
East Sussex.

Nature Conservancy Council,
73a High Street,
LEWES,
East Sussex

Countryside Commission,
John Dower House,
Crescent Place,
CHELTENHAM,
Gloucestershire

National Trust,
c/o Scotney Castle
LAMBERHURST,
Kent

For nature reserves in Kent and Sussex:

Kent Trust for Nature Conservation,
P.O. Box 29,
MAIDSTONE,
Kent.

Sussex Trust for Nature Conservation,
Woods Mill,
HENFIELD
West Sussex.